# SKIN

*A Matter of Race in America*

D1258475

# A. P. Brooks

**Seraphina Press**

Copyright © 2004, 2007, 2012
Seraphina Press, Jonesboro, GA
All rights reserved.

ISBN-13: 978-0-9857454-0-0

# DEDICATION

Nothing that is as timely as writing a book can be done without the love and support of family. This book was written in loving memory of my lovely mother Ernestine and step-father Lewis. To my awesome husband, Michael, and to my talented children Sheraun & Elijah. Also to my beloved grandchildren, Destiny and Kevin Jr. who inspire me. Thanks to my sister Janice; brother Reaman Jr.; sis-in-law Felisha; and all my dear family and friends who have supported me throughout the years. In memory of my dad Reaman Price who died when I was very young. Thanks to my parents *in the Spirit*, Pastors Ronald and Collette Gunby.

# ACKNOWLEDGMENTS

**Special thanks to:**
Joel Walker, Education Specialist, U.S. National
Archives Southeast Region
Todd Lamkin, Director of Collections Services, Michael
C. Carlos Museum at Emory
Petrie Museum of Egyptian Archaeology, University
College in London
Briana Pobiner, The Human Origins Program,
Smithsonian Institute
Damon Dozier, Director of Public Affairs, American
Anthropological Association
Sherry Turner, (first fruits)
Jeffrey F. Cox, Language Arts Instructor, Jonesboro
High School
Evelyn Everett, Clayton County Primary Teacher
Evan Savage from Sierra Leone
Anam Ajeroh from Nigeria
Laura Astacio, Brilliant graphic designer

*And* to Gerta, my dear German friend.

# SKIN

*A Matter of Race in America*

## INTRODUCTION

When I was very young, someone once told me "curiosity killed the cat." While growing up, my thoughts often rested upon this saying. Fear washed over me as I wondered, "Should I harness my curiosity?" And if not, would something bad happen? But it was impossible to control the constant inquirer living inside me and as it turns out, that was a good thing for curiosity has expanded my learning and understanding of other people and their societies.

Topics that were most stimulating to me even as a young child were those involving history or social matters. Reflecting back, I can remember the impassionate moments of watching President Kennedy's funeral on the black and white television or the day of Martin Luther King's funeral and the gray gloom that filled the air. I wondered why both events had occurred. My curious little mind never allowed me *not* to question such circumstances.

Part of the dynamics of my upbringing was race based on skin color - yet another curious circumstance. My parents never spoke about race in a differential way but within the broader community, there was always a preference given to people who were a rung or two up the ladder in a lighter skin tone or had a hair type closest to that of white people. Needless to say, my curious little mind wondered "Why?" and that curiosity has undoubtedly let to my writing this book. Still, *SKIN* did not initially begin with a commentary on race but on the origins of language. We all have a vocabulary deriving from somewhere and like DNA our words have their own kind of encoding with strands leading back to earlier times. Writing *SKIN* would begin with the science of etymology, which is the study of the birth and development of words. Following certain languages, a course was set for movement, history progression and finally the comparison of timelines, resulting in a chain of events leading to the development of race as it relates to skin color.

It is my sincere hope that after reading *SKIN* you are encouraged to join a new conversation about race in America.

**May the eyes of your understanding be enlightened.**

# Contents

# SKIN

*A Matter of Race in America*

A. P. Brooks

# Chapter I

# Makings of an Ideal

# THE INCEPTION

*Race* as we know it today. It defines, as well as, divides us. Furrowed deep within the contour lines of our racial perceptions are social nuances we ascribe to every stroke of skin color. We afford to race the power to decide human intelligence, beauty and even moral goodness. We have created a truth or at least, a reality to every shade of skin. Race can affirm or deny. It is a measuring rod, determining who is good or bad and whom we should hate or revere. For almost as long as our inception as a nation, Americans have worn these attitudes like a favored old garment with each generation providing fecund to keep it going. This is not to say that our social biases are insular. On the contrary, ideals like these have existed in societies around the world and throughout history, we find a shared consorter of sorts. One not necessarily connected to skin color, but nonetheless, torn from the same broadcloth and extending from the same thought process. Such ideals have caused great divisiveness; building walls of separation between people within a society and the reasons are as age old as class, religion, and geography – a big fuss over a little piece of land. And history shows us all too well, how one voice ratcheting up fury over one of these ideals can lead to mass violence. Certainly, such social intolerances exist anywhere there is a lack of compassion and understanding. Still, Americans do hold a distinction in this area. To be sure, our use of race based on skin color as a means to hate and discriminate, even more so, as an evolutionary benchmark is a uniquely modern concept.

Black, white, brown, yellow, and red are the monikers we use to describe race. These verbal expressions only fully indoctrinated into American society in the mid-1900s. During that time, there was a sweeping cultural embrace of white skin as evidenced by "free, white and over 21," a popular saying of the era, which supposedly, embodied the American ideal. An ideal that was explicit. For white skin was the litmus test for beauty and success and believed far superior to the darker hues. Obviously, this ideal was alienating to people of color especially for blacks. While it served as a bootstrap, a positive affirmation and a leg-up for white Americans, the result was altogether different for black Americans. In black neighborhoods all across the country "free, white, and over 21" parlayed into another just as popular but albeit, less affirming phrase: "if you're white, you're right, but if you're black, get back." Certainly both phrases were indicative of the times however, from the standpoint of a free democracy, this ideal seemed counterintuitive to what the U.S. Constitution stands for, that is, "We the people." Does it not mean *all the people*? One would think so; and if so, then decidedly, one group of citizens should not feel a sense of entitlement, based on their skin color, over others. Certainly, the U.S. Constitution does not appear to support such a claim for it makes no mention of race when defining citizenship. Instead, it affords the same rights and privileges to all citizens. Likewise, when the Declaration of Independence boasts of inalienable and equal rights of "all men," it makes no distinction to race. Nevertheless, this way of thinking continues to have strong implications on our society, creating barriers between American citizens.

Here in America, as well as in other societies where racial constructs were imposed, skin color matters a lot. But if we travel beyond western influences to view the matter of race from a global perspective, we find that in cultures around the world, skin color has no meaning. To the greater number of people on the planet, race based on skin color, counts for nothing. This makes our notions about race rather isolated. So then, the question becomes "Why do *we* place such emphasis on a person's skin palette?" Why abdicate human worth to skin, a part of the body that is as thin as a sheet of paper, serving as little more than a veil? Though these questions may sound challenging, nevertheless, they deserve our attention. To find answers, let's take a historical purview.

# THE MYTH

Race as it relates to skin color means "distinct species." More simply put, it is the separation of humans into sub-categories. Comparatively, we do not separate any other species in this same manner. For example, flowers are flowers and though they may differ in appearance, "a rose by any other name..." is still a flower with an array that is no less important than any other flower. Some would believe that separating humans into sub-categories has scientific support but that assumption is incorrect. Truthfully, there is no scientific proof that exists (based on pure scientific method) which backs up dividing people into racial categories. No proof at all. This means that our ideals about race are nothing more than false adulterations with no real value.

Decidedly, there is nothing *natural or scientific* about the concept of race. Nonetheless, many of us continue to hold on to these views as though they were indeed, fact. So hard-wired are we towards our ideas about race that many will go to the grave rejecting anything less. It is like the old Hans Christian Anderson story, *The Emperor's New Clothes* where the entire village was convinced in believing in something that even their own eyes proved wrong. So it is, that in the absence of truth, the greatest influence shapes reality. We likewise allow others to dictate what to think about race and as a result, shape our reality. When meeting someone for the first time, too often, we see skin color and what it denotes rather than getting to know the person's character. This propensity to form an opinion based solely upon skin color continues to cause an unending divide; and, if history bears out, a nation that holds to such destructive ideals will not long endure.

# THE MOTIVATION

Whether or not our racial concepts began out of a well-laid plan or if stumbled upon, the idea of separating humans into categories would develop its own specialized form of brutality. Many of us can point to the Trans-Atlantic Slave Trade as one influence in the development of race as a social concept. During this era, Western European nations captured and enslaved African people, transporting them to the Americas and Caribbean Islands. As the slave trade grew, within these slave-trading societies a new way of racial thinking began to develop. However, no one would be as adept at fine-tuning this racial thinking as the British.

For many generations to come, the Trans- Atlantic Slave Trade removed millions of African people from their homeland. Dispersed throughout the south, these Africans brought with them the knowledge of growing many types of crops. Their hands harrowed out what was once wild and untamed land into agricultural farms to build America's first economy. It was in this servile climate that plantation owners, benefiting from free labor, helped form laws that would govern the nation.

So it came as no surprise that they would subsume within the laws, racial disparities. Thus, with the stroke of their pens, America became the first great nation in history to separate people living in the land by skin color.

As time passed and the institution of slavery became more rooted in American society, over in England, the British were beginning to distance themselves from the slave trade. After gobbling up massive amounts of profits for centuries, the British suddenly became advocates of its demise. Denouncing the slave trade, the British ceased all involvement with trafficking Africans as slaves. Soon thereafter, neighboring nations followed suit. Each nation/state ended its formal involvement in the slave trade, all that is, except one. America was the lone holdout. On the surface, the abandonment of the slave trade by Europeans seemed noble and yet, their true intentions later became apparent. For each would play a clandestine role in furthering the demise of Africa and its people, using race to aid their cause. There is little doubt that Trans-Atlantic trade played an important role in the development of the concept of race. Still other causes may have attributed even more to the creation of this concept. To gain a better understanding, we must delve back in time, into the places and intersecting events that have influenced us. Like gazing into a dim mirror and seeing reflected back, day-gone-by eras that reveal where it all began.

*"Those who cannot remember the past are condemned to repeat it, "-* George Santayana, *Reason in Common Sense*

The creation of *race as a social concept* finds its beginnings in much the same way, as do many monumental events in history, in an act of obscurity. It begins with a tiny, insignificant flea. But before the flea, we must travel back to an even earlier time and place. Our journey starts in Africa.

# Chapter II

# Lost Ages of Africa

SKIN- 12 -

# THE AKKADS

This saga begins with a people whose lives have almost been erased…their stories, buried beneath the sand grains of the Sahara…their existence having faded into the eons of time. Many millenniums ago, there were mass migrations of people across the broad expanse of the mighty African continent. They traveled from place to place, settling wherever the land gave them the best provisions. Finally, reaching the northernmost crest of Africa, they crossed over into Asia to settle in the fruitful lands of the Mediterranean.

The Akkad people were among the first to make this grand journey to the Mediterranean, making their abode in the land of Sumer. The Akkads brought with them language, culture and technology, which was shared with the people of Sumer and their presence in the land sparked growth. New cities began to develop and the economy boomed. This coming together of the Akkadians and the people of Sumer was peaceful, without war or invasion. As populations grew, the people stretched forth their habitation beyond the land of Sumer, spreading throughout the foothills and pasturelands of the Mediterranean. In the beginning, they were little more than large extended families but as they added to their numbers children, servants and the like, they began to break off into tribes bearing the surname of each family. Overtime, each tribe developed distinct customs, traditions, and speech. From tribe to tribe, dialects branched off forming new variations of the old. It was like a marvelous tributary of spoken word flowing in every direction. The land pulsated with these diverging tongues to push lingua forward. You see, language is transitional and as a society changes, so too will language rearrange in both syntax and style. But no matter how much a language may alter, it will always bear a single origin.

In the Mediterranean, people spoke Hebrew, the language of the Jews and Aramaic, the language of Jesus Christ as well as many Arabic tongues. Each of these dialects grew out of Africa's tree of languages. Africa is the mother of them all. Even the Phoenicians, who invented the alphabet, spoke in a tongue closely related to Hebrew.

As their numbers grew, they germinated across the world setting into motion culture, economics, languages and finally, nation building. Yet no matter how far their journey would take them or what they would become—the essential part of them, the part they could never erase, would always lead them back to Africa: For we know that language follows its people.

# THE GARDEN

The growth occurring in the Mediterranean eventually spilled back into northern Africa and into the land of Egypt where a magnificent economy thrived. At the heart of this African civilization was the Nile River. Regions surrounding the Nile were lush and rich, even more so than that of the Mediterranean for the land of Egypt was known as the "Garden of the Lord." As the land continued to prosper, Egypt developed into a magnificent empire and because of its longevity, it is arguably, the greatest empire the world has ever known.

Now, if Egypt was God's garden, then the Nile River had to be His water spring, for people from everywhere were drawn to its delta. In time, Egypt became the center of world commerce. This constant influx of people and culture inspired creativity and the diversity, making the land a quintessential melting pot. Egyptians however, stayed true to their African heritage, maintaining the traditions and Coptic languages that originated out of Africa.

For many thousands of years, Egypt remained the

center of civilization. Their advancements in engineering, math, architecture, astrology and writing, show us how magnificent they were; and, the essential role they played in human progress. These people represented some of our greatest accomplishments and did so while wearing many shades of skin. To them, race based on skin color, had no significance at all. Nor did they equate skin color to what a person could or could not achieve.

# EGYPTIAN ACCOMPLISHMENTS

The tranquil bleating of sheep and well-tilled farmland gave no indication of the explosive innovation that was taking place in Egypt. Advancements made by these early Egyptians in math and engineering, were light-years ahead of anyone of their time, surpassing many kingdoms to follow. Still today, we are witnesses to their artwork, architecture and writing, created as many as four thousand years ago. We can stand at the foot of the Egyptian pyramids that tower above the dusty plains of El Giza as testaments to their ingenuity. Many would be surprised to know that early Egyptians built the largest pyramids thousands of years before the construction of the Greek Parthenon and longer still before handiwork to the Roman Coliseum was applied. In fact, these pyramids were built thousands of years before **any** major foreign influence had entered the land. Not only did early Egyptians make these achievements well before Greek and Roman civilizations ever existed but the empire would endure for over three thousand years, lasting longer than both the Greek & Roman empires.

What was both astonishing and fascinating about

these early Egyptians was that they were able to build these pyramids using materials that were not indigenous to the El Giza plain. Consequently, they had to transport thousands of tons of limestone and granite from rock quarries located far away. One wonders how they succeeded in hauling such large amounts of heavy stone especially without the aid of modern equipment. At the quarry, workers were lowered into the shafts and with the use of crude tools, they cut away thousands of pounds of stone. After loading up their huge cargo, they made the painstaking trip back to the El Giza site. Then stonecutters chiseled away two million stone blocks, each weighing as much as a ton. With basic hemp pulleys, they managed to put tons of stone into place to build Khufu, the largest and earliest pyramid. From its base to the tip, Khufu stands at least 481 feet high and 755 feet wide. Everything about Khufu as well as the other Giza pyramids was done intentionally for astrologers purposely aligned them with the four directional points of the earth and with Orion's constellation of stars. These early Egyptians understood the heavenly constellation and knew that the earth was round — knowledge Europeans still had not grasped thousands of years later.

Not only were they adroit in mining limestone and granite but also gold and fine gems like onyx, rubies, topaz, turquoise, sapphires, emeralds and amethyst.

Egyptian metallurgists prepared gold for furniture, and suffused zoomorphic idols in gold as well as onyx. There were lapidaries who cut beautiful gemstones into fine jewelry. All these worldly possessions were highly regarded by Egyptian royalty, so much so, they believed that in death their treasures could go with them into the afterworld. In keeping with this belief, when an Egyptian royal died, their possessions were buried with them in the cavernous tombs of the Valley of the Kings. But if they truly believed that in death, they could drink from a favorite chalice, the truth was made apparent with the passing of time as their possessions tarnished and disintegrated in the tomb.

To be sure, early Egyptian people were highly advanced but to some their identity is marked by skepticism. Still today, people muddle over who-they-were as though it was some grand mystery, needing to be figured out. But such perplexity is within itself, strange. One would think that since Egypt is in Africa, the natural conclusion would be that early Egyptians were indeed African. More interesting still is that when discussing civilizations such as Greek and Roman the same kind of pushback is not evident but rather, their European ancestry is readily accepted without the need to legitimize their identity. In addition, the marvelous contributions made in these lands are attributed to none other than the people that lived there, namely, the

Greeks and the Romans. So why then is there a question about early Egyptians and their African authenticity? In contrast, if we traveled to Africa, we would not find the same uncertainty about early Egyptians. No, Africans are quite clear on the matter. This means that the question of their identity only resides on our side of the fence. In any case, there is no need to ponder who-they-were for early Egyptians tell us. Fortunately, for us, they have left behind a dowry and within it is contained a roadmap to guide us along with artifacts that tell us who they were.

# EGYPTIAN IDENTITY

Through their artwork, architecture and writings, early Egyptians reveal themselves. Their identity can be seen in four-thousand- year-old paintings strewn across cold tomb walls in isolated sanctums. Housed with the sarcophagi, are colorful paintings, which tell their story. Paintings that show children at play, farmers at work and soldiers in war. Set in stone reliefs, the lives of royalty play out like still shots. Their artwork, like the pyramids, held a distinct purpose. The masterfulness shown in their paintings was intentional—to bolster a feeling of excellence among the people. They infused timelessness into their artistry in hopes of being remembered. They wanted future generations to know them. They wanted posterity's children to gaze and wonder. Their artwork shows how stylish they were, especially the young. Like teens today, they paid close attention to their looks. Young men and women wore well-coiffed braids and dressed in crisp white linen, which fit their slender bodies to perfection. From head to toe, they adorned themselves in jewelry. Worn around the neck was a gold cylinder-shaped pendant embedded in gems. Gold armlets snaked around their forearms.

Their wrists and ankles were embellished with golden bangles. Stunning in appearance, their skin was as brown as dried Ethiopian coffee beans.

Who early Egyptians were is seen in the statue of Princess Nefertiabtet. She, too, wore braids but in a more elegant style. Her braids fell to her shoulders in a symmetric cut and formed a crescent across her forehead. Her dress, made of a silky fabric, complimented her curvaceous body. Princess Nefertiabtet's skin was a rich brown, like butterscotch. The Egyptian culture and characteristics can be seen in a limestone statue of Sekhem-ka, a prominent man in early Egyptian times. While seated, a small child rests at his feet, which in those days symbolized the importance of family. His body, darkly painted, appeared like the bark of a Lebanon cedar. Early Egyptians show their faces in the statue of Prince Rehotep and his wife Nefert. Seated on a throne of stone, the prince's hair is styled in a neatly trimmed afro. Wrapped around his torso is a short white skirt and a simple necklace garnished the neck. Nefert, his wife, also preferred braids but added a pretty headband as an accent. Her long sleeved white gown exposed a beautiful neckline and smooth shoulders. Then there is the bust of Narmer, the very **first** Pharaoh of Egypt. In all of his kingly glory, he reflected an African heritage, thus, it is not hard to imagine that his skin color was dark, like

African blackberries. These early Egyptians were part of a longstanding succession of dynasties responsible for the Khufa pyramid as well as other great edifices. They are the ancient ones in whom the morning star kissed and saturated in radiance; what's more, their skin drank of its rays, as though it was the elixir of life. They found satisfaction and pride in their dark exteriors – dark like African earth. Skin color had no significance to them but they celebrated their African and Egyptian heritage. Today, their identity lies in knowing that they were black.

# TWILIGHT YEARS

One telltale sign that marks the demise of an empire or a nation is the constant wearing down of powers from within and Egypt would be no different. Inward feuding eventually weakened the empire leaving it vulnerable to foreign invasion. A succession of invaders attacked the land rather swiftly. Like birds swooping down upon prey, the enemies of Egypt descended upon the land. First, the Carthaginians and then the Persians. Next were the Macedonians, Greeks and finally, the Romans; all invaded Egypt within a short period of time and before the birth of Christ (B.C.). Not until hundreds of years later (A.D.) would Arabs invade Egypt, gaining lasting control over the land. None of these foreign invaders would be interested in keeping the legacy left behind by early Egyptians for it was customary in those days that conquering nations, as a show of strength, wipe the slate clean of the land's former inhabitants. So they destroyed many artifacts and written materials, tearing the people away from their brilliant past. Over the course of time and in the face of change the marvelous contributions made by these black Africans faded away and almost everything linking them to their glorious past was gone. The culmination of these events adversely affected the descendants of Africa for generations to come. As their history was blotted out, it was replaced with new articulations molded by foreign voices. Non-descendants who did not think it was robbery to take the advancements made by a greater nation and make them their own. Egypt's metamorphosis was complete.

# AFRICA SURVIVES

The upheaval in Egypt spurred on changes within the regions of West Africa. South of the Saharan desert, there was yet another African empire emerging to position itself within the borderless regions of the Sahel. What had occurred long ago in the Mediterranean and along the Nile in Egypt was once again happening at the River Niger. Not to be out done, the black cottony soil that surrounded the Niger was just as rich and fertile as was its predecessors. It was at the River Niger, the second longest river in Africa, that people began to converge in large numbers and their activities promoted growth in the area.

Now the flow of the Niger begins at the southernmost coast of Africa, meandering upward rather than downward for thousands of miles and through various terrains, until it reaches the northernmost point just shy of the savanna plain. Then it abruptly changes course. Forming into an oxbow, the Niger flows downward again and ends at the Gulf of Guinea, which spills into the Atlantic. For the people of West Africa, the River Niger was their greatest asset for the Niger meant *life*. In the same way as had the Mediterranean and the Nile, the Niger represented growth and civilization, fueling an economy that eventually grew into the West African Empire. Like Egypt's tradition of dynasties, the West African Empire was led by a succession of kings who ruled over the kingdoms of Ghana, Mali, and Songhai for several centuries. This empire stood united by twelve major states and thousands of minor territories and at its peak, encompassed a territory that spanned as far south as the Gulf of Guinea and as far north as the Sahara desert.

# AN EMPIRE RISES

What was most essential to the wealth of the West African empire was an elaborate system of small trading posts that ran along the vertical belt of the Niger attracting people from all over, in particular to the area surrounding the oxbow. Here, the land teemed with settlers to such a degree that it grew more populated than any other place south of the Sahara. From these small settlements came three major cities: Timbuktu, Djenne, and Gao. Each city was strategically placed along the fringes of the Sahara, serving as gateways to trade.

In Egypt's heyday, the people were known for their skill in architecture but this new African kingdom became famous because of trade, especially in gold. They were the juggernauts of the gold trade. Success in this trade hinged upon their ability to manage thousands of well-placed trade routes leading from the gold mines to trading posts along the Niger. Webbing throughout the western half of Africa, these trade routes were obscured by heavy brush, making them difficult to find and hard to travel. These routes were also well protected by patrols.

The regions of Mali, Ghana, Niger, Burkina Faso, Guinea, and Cote d'Ivoire were the richest in gold. Salt, another popular export, was found in parts of Niger, Burkina Faso, Mali, and Guinea. Rare ivory came from Cote d'Ivoire. In addition, diamonds, limestone, iron, and copper mines were scattered across several regions. Undeniably, this African empire possessed an over abundance of resources. When we consider all of its concentrated wealth, it is easy to conclude that the empire was the richest place in the world in natural resources and there is more. Within the belly of West Africa there is marble, granite, manganese, gypsum, uranium, titanium, chromate, nickel, cobalt, bauxite, platinum and petroleum oil; all of which fell under the control of the West African empire. Rulers however, kept their focus on gold - its excavation and transport across the Sahara into Egypt and on to Mediterranean trade ports. From there, gold was exported to faraway lands in Asia and Europe. This was the Trans-Saharan Trade System. Amazingly, this West African empire successfully transported huge amounts of gold across the entire brow of the Sahara. It was a feat, which mesmerized the nations.

# TRANS-SAHARAN TRADE

The very thought of crossing the scorching Sahara desert was considered by most, a moment of insanity. What was so frightening about the Sahara was its size. The largest dry dessert in the world, it stretches from one end of Africa to the other, filling up at least three million square miles. The Sahara is so wide that it literally slices Africa into two whole parts cutting off the north from the south. The vastness of the Sahara was so intimidating that even the most adventurous deemed it impassable; and rightly so, for the sand drenched terrain dangerously lacked food and water. Yet Saharan traders did cross and in droves. These desert frontiersmen made the seemingly impossible trek out of West Africa, all the way to Egypt, countless times. What's more, they traveled with as many as a thousand camels in tow; loaded down with tons of gold as well as other fine goods.

The camel, as a vehicle of transport, was flawless for its anatomy allowed it to withstand the desert extremes. Oversized hoofs attached to long slender legs looked awkward but were perfect for treading on the collapsible desert floor. Flaps of skin sealed off the nose, thick bushy hairs covered the ears, and long brush-like lashes guarded the eyes from the desert storms that whipped sand into a frenzy. What's more, the camel kept hydrated by preserving water in its hump, unlike Saharan traders who were not so well equipped. To save themselves from dehydrating, they relied upon their instincts to find hidden aquifers and basin pools. They protected their bodies from the blazing heat of the sun by layering in fabrics, which they often dyed for tribal distinction. One of the most distinctive dyes used was indigo, worn by Indigo tribesmen. With their swarthy skin tone and electric blue clothing, they appeared like guardians of the desert and the brilliance of their blue indigo stood out against a vacuous desert backdrop.

# TIMBUKTU – CITY OF COMMERCE

The city most pivotal to Saharan trade was Timbuktu for it stood at the very border of the desert serving as the portal for West African trade. From here, rulers controlled commerce, collecting taxes on exports as well as goods produced within the empire. Taxes were paid with gold dinars and other metals shaped like coins. In some regions, people used wood carved into small figures as currency.

*"King Askia was certainly the equal of the average European monarchs of the time and superior to many of them "* - Heinrich Barth, German explorer, Travels and discoveries in North and Central Africa

Since Timbuktu was the center for trade, it was a gathering place for cultural diversity, making it essential for West Africans to become polyglots. Having the ability to communicate in several different languages, especially Arab tongues, given Egypt's importance to trade.

The relationship between North Africa and West Africa through the buying and selling of goods would last for many centuries. For so long, the Saharan desert had stood in the way of these two diverging *Africas* but now trade brought them back together again, reconnecting them as kinsmen.

The most marvelous aspect of the Saharan trade was the tremendous wealth that rulers made from exporting gold and other fine goods while needing few imports. Because the empire was so rich in natural resources, it was essentially, self-contained. Therefore, there was little need to buy goods from other lands. Thus, what the empire dominated, other lands wanted. It supplied vital resources to other nations and not the other way around. Rulers needed only to keep control over the land while gathering unlimited amounts of wealth. Because of these seemingly perfect set of circumstances the empire drew the interest of other nations.

Wealth from trade allowed West African leaders to spare no expense in building their palaces. In fact, one king sent for an architect from Spain to build his palace, which was as large as a football field. Kings and other royalty wore special clothing made of fabrics designed by private *sartors*. Their special attire included kente cloth for Ashante royalty and bogolanfini cloth for Bambara chiefs.

# TIMBUKTU – CITY OF LEARNING

The hustle and bustle of trade caused a wonderful blending of languages and cultures. These interactions awakened ideas. In response, learning centers began to crop up all over the city of Timbuktu. Book supplies for these schools came from the north and overtime, books became one of the empire's largest imports.

*"In Timbuctoo there are numerous judges, doctors and clerics all receiving good salaries from the king. He pays great respect to men of learning. There is a big demand for books in manuscript, imported from Barbary (North Africa). More profit is made from the book trade than from any other line of business."*- Leo Africanus, Moor Scholar, 16th Century

Of all the learning centers in Timbuktu, the most prestigious was the University of Sankore. World renowned for its education, students came from faraway lands to learn at Sankore.

*"The scholars of Timbuctoo yielded in nothing to the saints and their sojourns in the foreign universities of Fez, Tunis and Cairo. They astounded the most learned men of Islam by their erudition. That these Negroes were on a*

*level with the Arabian savants is proved by the fact that they were installed as professors in Morocco and Egypt. In contrast to this, we find that the Arabs were not always equal to the requirements of Sankore."* - Filix DeBois, *Timbuctoo the Mysterious*

The large number of books being imported by West Africa was, in itself, a phenomenon for in those days most societies were illiterate. Thus, in these early stages of reading, it was an unusual occurrence that books were being introduced to West Africa by way of Trans-Saharan trade. Still, it was not the first time that cultural exchange through trade had incited learning for long ago in both the Mediterranean and in Egypt, foreign interactions through trade had sparked an explosion in learning. This tells us that when there is peaceful exchange of knowledge, new horizons of learning are reached and when cultures collide, ideas flourish. But the advancements made by these civilizations had taken hundreds and even thousands of years to achieve. In West Africa however, books were just beginning to be introduced and though such learning primed them for the same sweeping changes, for now, reading was limited to the wealthiest and most prominent. Beyond that, there was no saturation so that most retained an oral form of learning and yet, it too, had its disciplines.

# COMMUNITY LIFE

Oral learning that was passed down through the generations had to be accurate and central to the community's survival. This collection of knowledge was entrusted to the elders for only they could tell of the old ways and lasting traditions that gave the people purpose. The elders also played an important role in raising children, helping to mold their identity. So after doing chores and having a little fun playing touch or racing pod boats down fast moving streams, young children sat quietly and listened to the elder's instruction. They would tell them, "free things decrease one's intelligence" and "life's difficulty builds character." Family members and others in the community reinforced these teachings.

A mother's role was a conventional one, that of main caregiver. She was the central voice for a child's learning, especially girls. Mothers gave hands on teaching within the strict confines of village life. Drawing them near at an early age, mothers taught their daughters good behavior, housekeeping, farming, and cooking. They encouraged daughters to marry someone with "good advantages" and admonished them if they were too aggressive for aggression was looked upon as unattractive in a woman. Mothers instructed their daughters to avoid offending others and to be thankful and gracious at all times. Such matters of etiquette included greetings like "Nne Nwa daku" which means, "A child's mother thanks you." In some places, a woman's greeting of 'hello' meant the same thing as 'thank you.' So that when she greeted you with hello, she was also saying, "I appreciate you" all in the same breath.

Boys received their upbringing from fathers and other males in the community. In the same way as young girls, their training was also premised by traditional roles. At an early age, boys learned how to provide and to protect their families. In the area of respect for women, young men were taught to admire them as nurturers and the life source of the community. For in the woman was carried the ancestral line of the people.

Dogon tribesmen showed their high regard for women with sculptures of expectant mothers, depicting them in all their glorious curves. In the years of puberty, young men learned *not* to look upon a girl's exterior features to define true beauty. Although a beautiful smile from a girl, interplayed by a twinkle in her eye, was too irresistible to deny.

To Yoruba men, the eyes were a woman's best asset. Believing that the eyes were windows to the soul, when creating their artwork, Yoruba men made the eyes oval shaped and disproportionately larger than any other part of the body as to capture a woman's essence.

When the time came for marriage, young men learned the ritual of courting. It involved the potential groom presenting gifts to the parents of the likely bride, followed by the payment of a bride price that was oftentimes costly. Nevertheless, the bride price was important for it showed that the groom was serious about his intentions. Even more, that he valued his bride. The groom also had expectations of his own. His ideal wife had to be dutiful in marriage, good-natured and had to provide him with a harmonious home life. Passion as we know it was not important in marriage but endearment, the abiding love, which makes the union a lasting one, was very important. Whether marriage, birth, or death, everything served a purpose and everyone had to follow the longstanding traditions so that their lives remained orderly, keeping away chaos. Many other traditions such as the celebration of the harvest and the poetic verse in war were part of their everyday lives. Mandinka warriors, who were beautiful balladeers, set their poetic verse to song. Like the voices of seraphim, you could hear their melodies from afar. The Mandinkas also had a tradition of physical fitness and they showed off their chiseled bodies in competitions and rivalries that primed them for war. There was always the tradition of music, expressed through the language of the drums, the dance and the song. These activities were not merely enjoyable pastimes but brought a sense of harmony to the people. The most lasting tradition of all was family; for, everything they did served to reinforce this connection.

# A RELEVANT AFRICA

Many Americans have come to know Africa by way of watching National Geographic documentaries and the images that probably stick mostly in the mind are those that show an impoverished people living in a bleak land. Others might base their knowledge on the continent from old Mutual of Omaha programs that ran during the 60's and 70's. Every Sunday, people gathered in front of their television sets to learn about animals in Africa but there was little regard shown to African people. Then there are fans of Tarzan movies that infiltrated theatres across America for over half a century. Such imagery has overwhelmingly dictated our understanding of Africa. Hardly, if ever, did they show the love and respect that most Africans hold for their family and community – traditions, which have kept them going for many thousands of years, long after, others have died out.

America's school system has also been bereft in teaching about Africa. Our learning institutions provide extensive history leading back to Europe but we learn very little about our connection to Africa. As a result, far too many Americans do not know what Africa's true relevance to human progress is. What we should know is that as early as 800 A.D., an aspiring empire could be found in West Africa, which included the prosperous cities of Timbuktu, Djenne and Gao. In the cities, people lived in stationary housing and unlike our square shaped homes; theirs were cylinder in shape with cone-like rooftops. Since wood was readily available, they framed their homes with wood, using plaster to fill in the walls and thatching materials for the rooftops. In size, cityscapes went from small communities to large metropolises and all were arranged with functionality in mind. There was a separate building made for sleeping quarters and there was a building made for daytime activities. A freestanding kitchen housed a hearth for cooking and there was a common area in the middle of town, serving as a community center. The kraal, a fence-like structure for livestock, was built away from human living spaces.

Mainly because of its sturdiness and pliability, the acacia *seyal* was a favorite wood used by the people. It was good building material and its sticky sap was strong enough to use as glue. The bark held medicinal properties and the wood burned well for fuel. In many ways, the acacia was an extraordinary tree, especially because of where it grew – in the dry dessert. Surrounded by withering brushwood, tufts of dry grass and parched soil beaten down to a powdery dust, the acacia grew splendidly as much as 40 feet tall, flaunting its size in a feeble environment. It draws its hardiness from a root system that plummets as far down as one hundred feet, tapping into natural springs below. Because the acacia flourishes in a barren place, it is a symbol of strength and endurance. It even has spiritual relevance for the Holy Bible refers to the acacia as the wood used by Noah to build the Ark. It was the wood, sanctioned by God, to build the Hebrew Tabernacle as well as the Ark of the Covenant. Yet its spiritual relevance and importance to the people still does not tell the whole story for the acacia is vital to the desert ecosystem. As the liquid of life flows upward through its veins, it opens wide its canopy, attracting creatures both big and small. Its limbs are a retreat for big cats like the jaguar, and the leaves are nourishment for the elephant and the giraffe. The tip of the leaves, bursting with sweet nectar, feeds the beetle and the ant. The acacia is truly the tree of life.

The acacia is merely one indication of the wonders of Africa. With all it contains, Africa is more profound than any other land mass in the world. Virtually every flora and fauna on earth calls Africa home. There is an overabundance of rivers, lakes and streams filled with rich minerals and all kinds of fish. In those days, there were fresh water wells found throughout the empire and fish was the favorite food eaten by people living near the reservoirs. Throughout the regions, there is the grandeur of towering waterfalls cascading over the precipices and crashing to the depths in thunderous crescendo.

The land's complex and transitory beauty is also revealed within the regions of West Africa. At the coast, ecru colored sands buffer the Atlantic and tall palm trees stand aloft with a windward bend. A little ways inland are lowland swamps where overgrown mangroves intrude upon the landscape. A husky mist sits heavily above the dark waters arousing an eerie feel. Along the tidal swamps, people grew rice, a staple food in the area. Further, along, the land changes into thickset forestry and exotic plants grow into impenetrable gardens. Moving into the hinterlands, tree-laden mountains reshape the scenery and closer to the Sahara, the land changes yet again, flattening out to expose wide savanna plains. Here, moisture sucks out of the air, making the climate hot and dry. Herdsmen live on the savanna, caring for their livestock of sheep, cattle and goats. They ate these meats in hearty stews or roasted them over a fire and what was leftover they dried and stored away for leaner times. Although people raised chickens, they were only eaten on special occasions. Few people raised pigs so it was not common to their diets. Greens, yams, and cassava for bread cakes were their side dishes. From cultivating rice to raising livestock, no matter where they lived, people made good use of the land.

The variety of foods found in Ghana and Djenne were unparalleled. There were plantains, palm kernels, cassava, cocoa beans, corn, bananas, green vegetables, pineapples, coffee, millet, potatoes, sugar and nuts.

*"The inhabitants of Ghana are very rich...grain and animals are abundant so that the consumption of milk and butter is considerable"* - Leo Africanus, Moor Scholar 16th Century

Fruits and vegetables grew so abundantly that women set aside small commercial gardens and sold their goods in the open market. Naturally crafty, women weaved baskets from flax and made jewelry out of copper, coral and cowry shells, which they sold at the market. Mende people held an artistic tradition as blacksmiths, forging metals into intricate shapes from gardening tools to the head busts of kings.

*"...here in the West African kingdom there are great numbers of artificers (skillful, artistic workers)..."* - Frances Moore, *Travels into the Inland Parts of Africa 1730*

In the city of Djenne, the big tradition was the Monday market, which ran for miles along the main thoroughfare. Famous for its size and variety, the market was filled with a multitude of items: grapefruits, oranges, pomegranates, coconuts, pumpkins, lettuce, tomatoes, yams, millet, wheat, barley, maze and other goods. Such a marvelous variety of food and fresh water made the people very healthy and strong.

# RELIGIOUS BELIEFS

The Trans-Saharan trade not only greatly affected learning but it brought from the north, a new monotheistic faith called Islam – the belief in one Divine God. Traditionally, West Africans believed in minor gods but they also held an awareness of a Supreme God and this belief was transcendental. People always remained open to new ideas as long as it did not interfere with the values they held dear. With this in mind, they readily accepted Islam. First, the leaders and then the rest of the population willingly followed. Before long, stone mosques with minarets scaling the treetops were commonplace within the empire, a pleasing sight for the weary sojourner. In time, Islam replaced many forms of idolatry and yet their idol worship never completely ceased to exist but continued alongside a belief in the Supreme God. Still, Africans were not alone in their worship of deities for the world was filled with idolatry. People in every society created idols in order to interpret both good and evil. It was their way of expressing fear and awe of what they saw in the world, which was oftentimes violent and fleeting. Idols explained the unexplainable. Looking toward the sky, they saw gods in heavenly places. Gods of the sun, the moon and the stars. Sometimes their superstition drove them to mollify these gods with animal and human sacrifices. Only the Jewish Faith had, for thousands of years, sustained a belief in one Divine God but even they at times strayed, intermingling their faith with images of Baal, Asher and the asherah pole. Christianity, another monotheistic faith, would grow out of the Jewish Faith and it was just beginning to change the religious landscape in the Mediterranean. Later, the Islamic Faith would get its start from Christianity. All three faiths are related, acknowledging the same God, but each interpret Him in a different way. In the Jewish Faith, God is Elohim. In the Christian Faith, He is Almighty God and His son is Jesus Christ. In the Islamic Faith, God is Allah.

Both Christianity and Islam spread across the world but would go in different directions. Christianity set a course from the Mediterranean to isolated parts of northern Africa. Then it continued to trek a course across southern Europe and on to the west. Islam traveled from southern Asia to Africa and made its way through the eastern parts of Europe.

# LEGENDARY ALKEBULAN

Thus far, the journey through Africa has merely revealed a snapshot of what this great continent has to offer. Ancient lore tells us that Africa was first known as Alkebulan, "a land of positive mind and positive attitude." Given the traditions that remain common in the land, this sounds like an accurate description. For African people continue to embrace the idea that everything should serve a greater purpose. Furthermore, that life's experiences should provide insight to help understand the human condition.

# ABSENCE OF WAR

Trade winds carried the stories about Africa's treasures to faraway lands. They were tall tales of gold nuggets lying scattered on the ground or sprouting up from the earth like legume beans. These stories reached the ears of those in Europe and Asia, stirring more attraction to the land. Everyone desired this famed gold for it epitomized riches beyond the imagination. Although such stories were exaggerations, there was no denying that an abundance of gold was confined within West Africa. The earth seemed enceinte with gold for the more they mined, the more it gave of its treasure.

To protect the wealth of the empire, rulers built an army made up of hundreds of thousands of warriors, foot soldiers and cavalrymen as well as expert spearman whose pinpoint range bested any sharpshooter. Boat patrols guarded inland waters for the greatest threat did not come from outside the empire but within its own borders. In fact, rulers had little concern for foreign invasion for the empire was protected on all sides by natural defenses. To the north, there was the impenetrable Sahara, which no army had ever crossed.

The journey alone took several months. In addition, the scarcity of food and water made any attempt futile. If by chance, an army did survive the desert, it would have been so exhausted by the journey that defeat was imminent. On the empire's western and southern borders was ocean coastline where no ship had ever landed. Finally, to the east, the vastness of empty plains, mountains and thick jungle was quite treacherous. With these natural fortresses in place, rulers were assured that the empire was protected from all sides against any outside threat. They were self-contained, wealthy and up to this point impenetrable. In the absence of major war and invasion, West Africans grew complacent. Their complacency however, was viewed by nations outside the empire, as vulnerability.

# Chapter III

# Early English Times

# THE CELTS

During these early medieval days, while West Africa enjoyed peace and prosperity, across the world in Western Europe people faced perilous times. The land of England was under the colonial rule of the Roman Empire and the inhabitants called themselves Britons and Celts—the *hidden people*. Later, they would be known as Anglo-Saxons.

*... "These [Roman veterans] had recently been settled in the colony of Camulodunum [English lands] and had been driving its inhabitants [English people] from their homes and throwing them off their lands, calling them 'prisoners of war' and 'slaves'...Furthermore, a temple erected to the deified [god] Claudius lay before the natives' eyes like a bastion of everlasting domination"* - Cornelius Tacitus, *The Annals: The Reigns of Tiberius Book XIV 61 A.D.*

There came a time when the *hidden people* grew intolerant of Roman oppression and constant encroachment upon the land, so they rebelled. But while they waged war with Rome, they also fought bitterly amongst themselves, brother against brother and clan against clan in the way of the barbarians. In appearance, they looked the same so to distinguish one from the other in battle, they branded their bodies with ritual markings. They savored the ritual of decapitation believing that the head of their enemy held special powers, which they could possess.

*"Among the Celts the human head was venerated above all else, since the head was to the Celt the soul, center of emotions as well as of life itself, a symbol of divinity and of powers of the other-world"* - Paul Jacobsthal, "Early Celtic Art" 1944

They offered up these decapitated heads to the gods and like a trophy, placed them on prominent display in their dwelling places for all to see.

*"They cut off the heads of enemies slain in battle and attached them to the necks of their horses...and they nailed up these first fruits upon their houses just as do those who lay low wild animals in certain kinds of hunting."*
- Diodorus Siculus, Greek Historian, 30 B.C.

If offering up decapitated heads to the gods was intended to make their lives better then sadly, it did not, for their lives remained inexplicably hard. For now, the Roman Empire maintained its stronghold on the English lands, leaving the *hidden people* to bear out their scorn.

# EARLY ENGLISH LIFE

The lives of English people were meager. It seemed as though they were forever on the brink of starvation so that a hungry belly was commonplace. Season after season famine persisted, making the harvest unpredictable. With little knowledge of cultivating soil, it was difficult for them to get a generous yield, so they eked from the soil what they could. But even when the yield was generous, the crops grown provided little nutritional value so that consequently, people were unhealthy.

The times pre-dated the bathroom so they dug a small pit some distances away from the home as a makeshift toilet and the fecal soil from the pit was used to fertilize their food crops.

Other than the *bosky* areas where trees were plentiful, people had to use wood sparingly, so they built their one-room cottages with *wattle*, which was a mixture of woven reeves and twigs. The roof of the home was a collection of straw and marshland materials that wore easily and thus, often needed replacing. Because wood was scarce, few people could build barns, so farm animals lived in the home among people. Their animals roamed freely, back and forth from human spaces to outdoors and to the *byre*, a small storage room for crops that was attached to the home by a narrow hall. The constant presence of animals in the home caused large infestations of insects. The shortage of wood also meant that fuel for cooking and heating water for cleaning was at a minimum. Such shortages in resources created a hostile environment.

Inevitably, the combination of poor diets and lack of fuel began to take its toll on the English. Their health degraded and the land was a breeding ground for disease. Childbearing was especially difficult and oftentimes both mother and child died during birth. Of the percentage of children that did survive, a great number of them bore a lifetime of handicaps, which added to their daily struggles. Yet remarkably, life found a way for the population of English sustained.

# NORMAN INVASION

The Normans were specialized in warfare. Filled with vigor and might, the very thought of war ignited their primal fury. Freebooting marauders, they scoured the land like a pack of wolves, searching for something to destroy or steal and always eager to shed blood.

*"...A very shrewd people indeed, quick to avenge injury."*
- Geoffrey Malaterra, *The Deeds of Count Roger of Calabria and Sicily and His Brother Duke Robert Guisc*, 11th Century

As warriors, the Normans were unrivaled in battle. Void of normal inhibitions, they fought as though overcome by madness. Life had no meaning in war and a death resulting from war was far better and honorable than to die in peace.

*"... They were enduring of toil, hunger, and cold whenever fortune laid it on them. Given to hunting and hawking, delighting in the pleasure of horses, and of all the weapons and garb of war ..."* - Geoffrey Malaterra, *The Deeds of Count Roger of Calabria and Sicily and His Brother Duke Robert Guisc*, 11th Century

Tales of Norman pursuits struck fear throughout the

land. Even their appearance was intimidating. In archetype, they were statuesque with muscular build. Their yellow hair was like a field of plumped wheat and their eyes were strikingly blue, as though dipped into the sea in which they journeyed. Always in search of a new home but once found, they turned away again in search of other conquests.

*"Scorning the fields of their homeland in hopes of acquiring something more. Avid for profit and domination..."* Geoffrey Malaterra, *The Deeds of Count Roger of Calabria and Sicily and His Brother Duke Robert Guisc*, 11th. Century

After several successful campaigns around Europe, Norman warriors came upon the land of the *hidden people*. By now, the Roman stronghold had dissipated leaving the land open for invasion. Embolden by past conquests, Normans set sail for the English shores. Like a band of mythical *jotuns* riding upon chariots of the sea, they ascended upon the ill-fated people and straight away, the land fell into the hands of Norman conquerors.

From conquest to conquest, the Normans continued their surge across Western Europe. After invading a land, they were careful not to disturb the customs already in place, believing that in doing so, the inhabitants would be less likely to resist their presence. Normans assimilated well within in these societies, readily accepting the customs in place and ridding themselves of their own hodgepodge beliefs. Because they were a nomadic people upon entering some of these lands, they were surprised to find stability and advancement, which made their conquests all the more rewarding.

*"Normans were specially marked by cunning, despising their own inheritance in the hope of winning a greater [one]. Eager after both gain and dominion. Given to imitation of all kinds..."* Geoffrey Malaterra, *The Deeds of Count Roger of Calabria and Sicily and His Brother Duke Robert Guisc,* 11th Century

When the English were under the colonial rule of Rome, they needed only to tolerate a few Roman settlements scattered throughout the land. However, the Normans moved in, taking complete control over the land and the people. The English could no longer own their own land and they were forced into pre-dial slavery, having to work the land without pay. Their condition was made even worse by the fact that Normans only spoke French, a language the English could not understand. Normans would rule over the English for centuries to come and like any bequeathal of property the people were passed down as pre-dial slaves, from one landowner to the next, always remaining attached to the land. Their status as pre-dial slaves was not contingent upon skin color but rather, origin.

Norman rulers lifted themselves to the level of nobility and lived lifestyles worthy of the title but kept the English destitute. The Normans, once nomads of the sea, would now shed their barbaric ways for culture and civilization.

*"The Normans chief men were especially lavish through their desire of good report. They were, moreover, a race skillful in flattery, given to the study of eloquence, so that the very boys were orators,"* Geoffrey Malaterra, *The Deeds of Count Roger of Calabria, Sicily, and His Brother Duke Robert Guisc,* 11th Century

Lastly, the English could no longer move freely about their land without first gaining permission from their noble master.

# A BURGEONING RELIGION

After taking control over the English lands, Normans were introduced to a burgeoning monotheistic religion called Roman Catholicism. Now the belief in One God was a entirely new experience for the pagan-entrenched Normans who loved their gods and goddesses as well as celebrations of the underworld. Even though they were steeped in idol worship, the Normans accepted this new faith albeit, their approval was probably more conciliatory than effectual. Eventually, many of their ancient practices converged with Catholic dogma.

It is difficult to say whether the cause for change resulted from Norman presence or the spread of Roman Catholicism but suddenly, the land of the English gained a heartbeat and began to flourish. The Normans had taken a different approach to leadership by forming levels of authority, which worked. They applied their skills as shipbuilders to city building and accommodated Catholic leaders by building the first churches in England; but this was not an indication that their relationship with the Roman Catholic Church was anything more that one of forbearance. Throughout this time of growth, the English remained among the lowest class and it seemed that as long as Norman nobles and Catholic leaders were in authority, their status was unlikely to change. Still, the Normans and Catholic leaders had their own problems to worry about for the nobles were in constant battles with other lands and Catholic leaders bitterly disputed over power.

# THE FLEA

The first indication was a cough. Under normal circumstances, a single cough will not elicit much of a response but at the time, it sent people into a frenzy and rightly so; for, if caught within an arm's reach of a noxious spray, meant you were contaminated. Once infected, the pathology picked up speed. A slimy mixture of saliva and blood seethed from the mouth. A smelly substance drained from the eyes, ears and other openings on the body. Lymph nodes on the neck swelled like giant furuncles and boils, filled with pus, bubbled up around the groin area. Death *paused*...as though awaiting the last blows of the disease - agonizing pain and a fever so high that it brought about the spectacle of madness. If there was any consolation to be had, it was in the swiftness of the disease, for it killed within a matter of days. What we know today as the Black Plague, they called "The Great Dying." Its arrival was tantamount to a death sentence in England as well as in neighboring lands. Without warning, the virus swept across the English countryside with the ferocity of a mighty whirlwind.

Dispatched upon a tiny weightless flea, the plague found preferable abode upon the meager black rat, an allusive and yet prolific creature that scuttled along dark alleyways in crowded conurbations. Carried by the black rat, the flea took up lodging with the farm animals and went unnoticed behind the walls of human dwellings. With its host the black rat, it stowed away on trade vessels that carried the virus to faraway places, dispersing it at every port. Wherever there was a convergence of people, the tally of dead increased. It blew from town to town, leaving a massive trail of death in its wake. Among the lands hardest hit were England, Italy, Germany and France. The virus spared few as it assailed over the young and old, the rich and the poor. It moved like a specter, unrepressed by false securities in locked doors and latched shutters. Indeed, it preferred such quarantined spaces that acted as incubators for the disease to spread more rapidly among family members. Utter fear of being contaminated caused loved ones to abandon the care of their family. Even priests and physicians, charged with the care of the sick and the dying, were too afraid to give aid.

*"...parents of kindred never visiting them... brother forsook another, the uncle, the nephew, the sister; and the wife her husband. Nay even much greater and almost incredible; fathers and mothers fled away from their own children as if they had no way appertained [belonged to] them."* - Giovanni Boccaccio, *The Decameron*, 1350

Because there was no cure, the Black Plague moved swiftly and irrepressibly to slay the nations.

The disease was particularly fastidious toward the people in England for more of them perished than in anywhere else in the world. Death came to the English with such frequency that bodies lay sprawled upon the cold cobblestone streets, awaiting the death wagon to scoop them up. The number of dead was so overwhelming that normal funeral and burial rites ceased. Instead, they dug deep holes in the ground and bodies were unceremoniously thrown in, one on top of the other, like an illuminator's depiction of hell.

*"And so because of the shortage of people to care for the sick and the violence of the disease, day and night such a multitude died that it would dumbfound any to hear of it who did not see it themselves"* - Giovanni Boccaccio, *The Decameron*, 1350

The most terrifying thing of all was the mystery behind the disease. Was it in the air or carried on the skin or clothing? No one knew and there was no place to hide. Among the noble class, there were murmurings that indeed, something vile was wafting about the air. So when entering public places, they pressed fragrant posies against their nostrils to either stave off the stench of death or to keep from inhaling something deadly. To most, it seemed that the whole world was contaminated and the Apocalypse was nigh. The totality of the number of English killed by the virus, on average, amounted to two thousand people per day. Unbelievably, as the virus rendered its deathblows both famine and war continued without interruption. Death was descending upon the English from all sides for if spared by the virus then famine or war was your ticket to the grave. Death moved among the people as though it were an entity competing for their souls. It stood beside the merchant selling his wares and the farmer gathering the grain. Death strolled along the busy marketplaces and sat with the assembly in the church abbey. In the evenings, it joined them at the dinner table. The enormous number of dead and dying pushed England toward complete disaster and finally the society collapsed. Everything came to a standstill. Authorities responsible for keeping order in the streets were gone. Thus, with wing-beat speed, mass hysteria spread across the land. Believing death could befall them at any moment people set aside good judgment for wild abandonment. Fear harnessed the flesh, unleashing primal desires and many were consumed by the most indecorous behavior imaginable. Ancient superstitions crept back in, so people looked for a transgressor - someone to punish for an unspecified guilt. It did not matter where the blame would fall: family, friend, or foe. Wherever there was a whispered allegation or an accusing finger, swift execution followed.

In the *shetl* towns across England, large groups of Jewish people lived rather autonomously, outside of mainstream society. Although they were citizens, their customs and mannerisms made them appear foreign to others. It was solely, by nature of their differences that Jews were singled out by people looking for someone to blame for all of England's woes. Thus, the Jews were made the *Azazel,* the chosen scapegoat for the virus. As a penalty, the English drove them from their homes and businesses and many of them were murdered. No longer welcomed in England and shunned as well in other western lands where plague was at its worst, the Jews were exiled into the wilderness. They finally found refuge in less populated regions in the east, leaving behind the crowded streets of England where at the stroke of the bell's clapper people died. It was just as well. The scarcity of people in their new land spared many lives from plague.

Yes, the times were extremely volatile in the land of the English. Still, most people looked to the Roman Catholic Church for help and guidance.

# THE CRY

Besieged by the cries of the people to end the pestilence and intervene on their behalf before God, the Roman Catholic Church instead, laid the blame squarely upon its followers. Their sin, Catholic leaders said, had caused the plague and only penance leading to forgiveness could save them. Yet obtaining forgiveness was not as easy as merely asking, for priests withheld their benevolence unless a material gift was in hand. To the greater number of Catholic followers living in abject poverty, these pecuniary obligations placed God's forgiveness out of their reach, which further actuated their guilt and despair.

The Roman Catholic Church, as a state religion, had full authority to punish anyone who followed another belief system. Furthermore, it forbade its followers from owning or reading the Bible, which left the extent of their spiritual edification up to the priests; but, even if they could have owned a Bible, it was written in Latin a language they could not understand. A language that priests were only allowed to learn. Consequently, their devotion to the Roman Catholic Church was one of obligation rather than a willing choice, which amounted to forced religion. What's more, when the priest delivered his sermon to the congregation, he did so completely in Latin, further hindering Catholic followers from learning the tenants of their own faith. Though the words they spoke were quite eloquent, the people were left none the wiser. Such circumstances made it impossible for people to gain relevant understanding about what or in whom they should believe. But there was one point that the Catholic Church conveyed loud and clear. It was the irrefutable authority of the Roman Catholic Church. Leaders would declare the Catholic Church as the **only** representation of God on earth. They would assert that the Catholic Church had within its possession, keys to the gates of heaven, which meant no one could enter into heaven without their consent. Essentially, priests alone had the discretionary power to grant salvation, forgiveness and redemption. In all their human frailties, they stood in judgment of a person's soul. This absolute authority greatly influenced the peasant population that made up about ninety percent of Catholic followers. Their devotion to the Catholic Church would result in a strong dependency upon the institution and leaders of the Catholic Church began to put into place certain sacraments, which people had to follow. There were rituals such as Penance and "Viaticum" or Provisions for the Journey for the sick and the dying which became part of their everyday lives.

Moreover, these rituals were made necessary to the saving of one's soul and only priests could administer them. Yet in the years of plague, such rituals said to be essential to salvation, altogether ceased.

To be sure, the Catholic Church did not totally disregard its followers for priests offered certain fineries to serve as conduits for their faith. Beautiful sculptures of the Virgin Mary and Jesus Christ as well as countless patriarchs were displayed in every abbey. These and other accoutrements held the interest of followers. Then there were theatre troupes that traveled from town to town and in the village square, performed plays that were loose renditions of Bible scripture. Albeit entertaining, these plays added little toward spiritual enlightenment. Maybe that was the point. To keep the masses ignorant and afraid, thus, powerless. The downside was that the more restrictions placed on followers by the Catholic Church, the more people depended upon the leadership. A dependency that grew quite burdensome during the plague for Catholic leaders were unable to help followers, even with the most basic spiritual needs. Indeed, how could they given the condition of the Roman Catholic Church.

# THE CONDITION

The authority of the Roman Catholic Church had risen above rulers of nations. Wielding power over both prince and peasant, it was now laid to waste by disease. Death struck on every ecclesiastical level rising to the heights of cardinal. The plague had wreaked such havoc upon the prelature that church abbeys stood deserted, like vacant grottos of the Divine. But there was yet another pestilence running amok within the four walls of the Roman Catholic Church. An epidemic that threatened its very existence. It was sin. Though leaders in the Catholic Church distinguished themselves as pillars of godliness, they were in fact, among the biggest offenders of sin. Their actions were as worldly and intemperate as those they were commissioned to save. The promiscuity of nuns and priests shrouded the Christian message and their sin went unchecked by higher authorities in the Catholic Church. They lived as lavishly as did kings, feasting upon the best delicacies and clothing themselves in the finest furs and jewelry. All the while the masses of followers suffered. Such neglect had to arouse contempt in the eyes of God. Catholic leaders were also stymied by greed. Rather than their usual conferring before deciding ministerial roles, they sold offices to whoever could afford them. For a larger fee you could buy *Indulgentia a culpa et a poena* or Indulgences. This was *gratis,* if you will, pardoning your sins, irrespective to how bad they may have been. It also kept you out of hell. Likewise, in the absence of repentance. The extent of their greed was shown as they seized excessive amounts of real estate in England, France, Germany and Italy. After which, they forced the peasants to pay them taxes that were oftentimes excessive. Resting upon their laurels, leaders in the Roman Catholic Church gathered up as much wealth as they could, while holding firmly within their grip, keys to the kingdom of God. The control over both mind and spirit of the people.

*"...the first and sorest was that she [Roman Catholic Church] loved money and had too much of it for her own good."* - Will Durant, *The Reformation* (The Story of Civilization VI) 14th Century

# Chapter IV

# The Teacher

SKIN- 76 -

# THE AFTERMATH

In the same abrupt way as it began, the plague suddenly ended. The death knell eased. Decades would pass before they discovered real causes for its onset but at the time, they attributed the reduction in infections to better sanitation habits introduced by the French. In the aftermath, there was hardly a footprint left of their former lives. Within a three-year period, plague had killed at least twenty five million people in Western Europe alone. The English towns of Tottenham, Haringey and Loughborough, where throngs of people once filled the winding streets, were deserted; as if, the earth had opened wide its mouth and swallowed up half the citizenry. Although the number of infections had decreased, the agony of what had taken place still lingered. Over Essex, Surrey, and Middlesex it hung like marshland fog, bearing down upon the meadowlands like a North Sea *haar*. For what seemed an eternity, survivors had been locked into a macabre dance with Death. The experience was so unspeakable that even the most ardent writer, placing quill to vellum, could hardly put into words. Plague had *trimmed the fat*, if you will, from the English. A *forced* population control that for a while relieved them of food shortages but it was a bitter consolation to those who had lost loved ones lost. Now the crop fields overflowed in anticipation for the harvest but unfortunately, there were not enough people to gather it all up. Thus, fields of crops withered on the vine if the rodents did not eat them.

Plague had greatly reduced the number of nobility. The highest class in the society had been decimated by disease such that consanguineous bloodlines were completely severed, leaving no male heir to carry forth the name. Even entire noble families were wiped out. The damage was so extensive that the role of nobility within the society permanently shifted; and, the noble class never regained its full power. Likewise, plague had forever diminished the authority and power of the Roman Catholic Church.

# FATES' REWARD

While the nobles and Catholic leaders scrambled to recapture their foothold on the land, the English had a better plan in mind. With the wind at their backs, pushing them toward a new destiny, the English believed the Fates were finally on their side. They had survived the horrors of plague, famine, and war. Although less in number, they looked forward to a brighter future. Distancing themselves from the mores of the past, which had held them back, the English began to think independently. First, they *laid bare* the Roman Catholic Church questioning its significance in their lives especially during the plague. Because of their discontent, they no longer looked to the Catholic Church for guidance, whether spiritual or otherwise.

After the plague, Catholic leaders were embroiled in a contentious battle between authorities. So while they worked out their differences, the English moved forward with less interference from the Catholic Church. Since the nobles now had limited authority, control over the land fell into the hands of the monarchs - kings and queens who were highly receptive to the needs of the English people. The major upheaval, which had just taken place, caused the land to be unstable and therefore susceptible to another invasion. A quiet desperation filled the English lands. If the people were going to survive, the time to unite and build was at hand.

Barring a few minor skirmishes, the English lands remained largely at peace. Thus, while neighboring nation/states were busy fighting each other the English focused their energies on nation building. What was most critical to their success was something they had never accomplished before, which was unity. For they had always lived separated by principalities and each township had developed customs, ways of governing and speech which was unique to that community. Indeed, for there was not a common language spoken between them. Neither was there a written language shared by all. When Normans ruled over the land, they brought some continuity to the language by joining the various English dialects with French with the latter serving as the dominant language. Now it was necessary for them to develop their own lexicon. A language shared by all English people.

As former restraints fell away, knowledge opened to a broader audience. These new seekers of learning had few allegiances to the Roman Catholic Church or the noble class. What began as a ripple grew into a wave and then a tempest. A new era of independent thinking had arrived. People no longer sought after the normal realms of authority for answers. Moreover, they began to distance themselves from the Roman Catholic Church. Undoubtedly, this grand exodus had resulted, at least in part, from a gross lack of understanding and connection to their faith. But their rejection of the Catholic Church seemed to have also included lessoning God's role in their lives for they removed Him from their day-to-day affairs, designating His role to that of onlooker. God would no longer have anything to do with their successes or failures. English scholars went a bit further by altogether rejecting His existence. They determined that the belief in God was motivated by fear and superstition. Moreover, they concluded that people could live a full and pleasant life without the interjection of God. To the English, God had become at most, *hands off* and at the very least, *unknowable*. Either way, removing God from their lives meant that matters of right and wrong would be theirs to interpret. This made the English people, *a god unto themselves*. But strong resistance to these ideas came from new forms of Christianity, unrelated to the Catholic Church. These new believers reverted to Gospel teachings that preached a personal God. Still, they had little effect on the policies made by leadership for in many ways nation building had become their religion.

# NATION BUILDING

Under the new rule of kings and queens, the English began to set a course for success. When the nobles ruled over them, learning had been an afterthought but monarchs understood how important knowledge and discovery was to nation building. The English, however, had some catching up to do for neighboring nation/states had already started making strides in advancement. To help expedite their goals, the English gleaned knowledge from the Germans and the French; acquiring more from Spain, Portugal, and Scandinavia. But their most essential knowledge, which ultimately led to their success, came from the ancient worlds of Greece and Rome. It was an interesting turn of events. For the Romans had always considered the English to be an inferior and barbaric people. Now the Roman civilization would be their greatest benefactor.

In order to unlock Rome's treasure trove of knowledge, the English had to become proficient in Latin, the language of intellectuals. So they called upon Catholic priests who were experts at translating Latin to help decipher ancient writings of some of the greatest philosophers, scientists and mathematicians of all times. The English disciplined themselves as students devouring this information and then supplanting it back into their society. Their passion for learning was unparalleled for they sought after knowledge as though seeking after a lost love. They would uncover such a large content of ancient works that some scholars wanted to re-publish them as standard learning. Still others devoted a lifetime to studying one discipline or another. All this learning had a marvelous impact on the English society. Latin would even play a key role in the development of modern English. Before long, a new breed of intellectuals emerged. They were inventors, mathematicians and philosophers who now represented the upper echelon of English society, lending the same level of eloquence to this status as had the nobles and Catholic leaders. The difference was that they actually contributed to the nation's progress.

To stimulate new discovery, monarchs offered monetary incentives, which kindled creativity. The land was abuzz with new ideas as though large vats of knowledge had poured down upon them. Ingenuity was highly encouraged as long as it benefited the nation's goals and if an idea was successful, fame was sure to follow. Knowing this, people pressed their way into the cities causing an explosion of activity. Yet the process of invention was not for the faint of heart because it involved rigorous research and experimentation. Day and night inventors toiled over complex theories, driving some to the edge of madness. But if an invention was awarded a patent letter, it made all the hard work worthwhile. In this fiercely competitive atmosphere, plagiarism was an issue, even with leaders who had a penchant for *borrowing* ideas originating from other lands. Still, to their credit, the English did not waste ideas but rather, put what they learned to good use.

# SHAKING THE TREE

After centuries of nation building, the English had lifted themselves out of generations of repression to a standard of living that epitomized high culture. A love for all things Greek and Roman was easily seen throughout the land. Norman gothic structures had been replaced by ancient classical styles. Façades on every formal building were enhanced with Greek architecture so much so, that English cityscapes appeared like the progeny of a dead civilization.

The economy had also transitioned from agriculture to industry. Business merchants replaced farmers. Factories with huge chimneystacks bellowing out smoke into the air gave work to the average proletarian. The English had developed a financial system based on banking methods in Italy and France. After shoring up their economy, they focused their attention on shipbuilding and weaponry advancement. In time, they built a fleet of merchant ships that were unsurpassed in speed and agility, which pushed them to the forefront of trade. Breakthroughs in weaponry made them "a force to be reckoned with." And by conscription, they built up a military force in the millions. For the English, necessity had truly been the mother of invention. They had discovered how to harness the earth's raw materials and to apply knowledge in more effective ways. But in the process of making these achievements, the English grew arrogant. Even to the degree that scholars believed they had laid all the groundwork for every field of study and there was nothing left to learn. The monarchs, as financiers of all this growth, also wallowed in their triumph for now, they ruled over a unified people and cooperative society. The people had become generational thinkers and every move they made was to preserve the English nation. This kind of forward thinking would keep them one-step ahead of everyone else.

The English had relentlessly shaken the tree of knowledge, eaten their fill, and was careful not to leave anything behind. What they did not know was that the most desirable fruit on the tree, the hidden part at its core, still remained.

The difficulties of the past were no more. They could now create a history that was more inclined to their current status and so the English began to romanticize their past. At this moment, life began to imitate art.

# A NEW IDENTITY

It had taken the English about four hundred years to rise from a low estate to a powerful nation. Like the phoenix, they had lifted themselves out of the funeral pyre to reveal something magnificent. But during this time of growth, a national attitude was formed, becoming the premise for the concept of race.

From the start, their efforts to build a nation were complicated by the devastation of the plague. A multitude of families were either displaced or left without breadwinners so that the chances of survival for women, children and the elderly were bleak. A staggering number of waifs, children left without parents, lived on the outskirts of towns. Communities looked like wastelands. Local parishes tried to help but too many people were in need to make a difference. The family unit was so fractured that out of necessity, hundreds of mutual aid groups - guilds, fraternities, labor parties and other social organizations formed across the land. These groups brought people together for a common cause and restored a sense of community. They acted as surrogates to the family providing comfort and encouragement. Like the breadwinner, they gave support to the family and in return, they required the same familial loyalties. Dependency upon them however, diluted the role of the traditional family, lessoning the need to develop strong family ties. What's more, most groups only gave aid when something of value was given in return. So that people with the greatest need such as the poor, women, children, and the elderly went without help. This was the subtle beginnings of placing value on people according to their usefulness. It was fertile ground for the development of ideals such as "survival of the fittest."

Having relegated God's role as bystander, the task of molding a national moral compass would be left to the philosophers and other learned men. People who had no interest in chasing *a cloud by day or pillar of fire by night*. Neither were they in search of a thunderous voice from a *burning bush*. God's role in their lives had become a matter of utility, which meant they could make Him into whatever they needed. Thus, the likeliest progression was to make God in their image and make Jesus Christ of Nazareth look like them having white skin, blonde hair and blue eyes, erasing all of his Jewish heritage.

To help mold a moral compass for the nation, the English once again reached back to ancient scriveners for guidance and found Epicureanism, a moral ideal made popular by the Greeks. Epicureanism defined moral goodness as the act of pleasing oneself. The greater the pleasure, the more morally good it was said to be. This principle appealed to English leaders for it allowed them to pursue every wanton pleasure without the pricking of their conscience. But embracing a moral ideal that focused entirely on self, made them appear selfish. To counterbalance this ideal, they added, *Quod tibi fiery non vis, alteri ne feceris* or "Do not that to others you would not have done to yourself." It encouraged giving to others but only when they have given to you. It also required that acts of giving be in equal measure to what you have received. As such, the act of giving had to be reciprocal in both proportion and selection. Such a principal made English leaders appear good and probably made them feel better but the intent still resided in self-centeredness. Clearly, this principle alluded to Bible scripture which says, "Do unto others as you would have them do unto you" (Luke 6:31). However, in scripture, the emphasis is placed on *giving* rather than *receiving*. Acts of goodwill are encouraged *first* and without limitations or the expectation of receiving something in return. This is the truest form of goodwill. Yet, the wheels were turning in a different direction.

# THE RIGHT PATRIOTISM

Success had hinged on two long-term objectives: (1) the preservation of the English people and (2) the ability to be self-sustaining. Becoming self-sustaining would come later. In the area of preservation, the English had proven their chameleon-like way of adapting to any situation had kept them going through the generations. But the many changes taking place over a short period had made it difficult for them to hone a clear identity. The task itself was daunting enough for it required shifting the mindset of an entire group of people, like two tectonic plates smashing together: old ways colliding with new ways until an identity emerges. Monarchs were interested in a national identity that required an unwavering loyalty to the British Crown. So they enlisted the help of scholars, who had benefited from their purse strings, to push a national identity in the context of a moral compass. Certainly, patriotism is important but what they advocated was extreme. It was a blind sense of duty to country above all else, which they characterized as a moral right that was inherently found in the English race. Rejecting this explanation of moral right meant you lacked character and you were deemed an enemy of the state. Once again, the rights of the people were slowly being taken away. Their choices were swallowed up by a grander mechanism of moving parts. Like a big wheel within a little wheel. The masses were the little wheel being steered by the big wheel, the leaders, in whatever direction they chose and at every turn, they boasted of their superiority.

Upon the arrival of the printing press, leaders immersed the land in printed materials filled with claims of superiority. The masses were captivated by these ideas. Eventually the English came to believe that they were the *will of God's laws* no matter what they did. With the masses thoroughly ingratiated in ideals of superiority, a national identity solidified. A xenophobic identity expressed through a national arrogance and deep disdain of others not like them. During these early stages of nation building, the concept of race had not yet developed but under these circumstances, it is easy to see how it could take shape. In this atmosphere of racial superiority, the English needed only to veer slightly to the left or to the right for it to manifest.

At certain intervals in history the Greek, Roman, and Egyptian civilizations built their kingdoms upon the backs of weaker nations. The British seemed poised for a similar fate.

# FOR GOD AND MY RIGHT

With the onset of the modern era, a marvelous time of exploration began as ships traveled from Western Europe, seeking shorter routes to benefit international trade. They also sought natural resources. First, the people of Portugal set sail to new lands. Then the Spaniards, people of the Netherlands, the French and finally the British. Though the British were among the last to journey to other lands, true to form, they surpassed everyone else in exploration. By now, the British population had built up again and concern centered on the nation's long-term sustainability. In their current land, they had little room to expand. In addition, the need for natural resources was a constant issue. Thus, the British, always the shrewd thinkers, masked their travels as mere exploration but in reality, they were gathering tactical information on the people, the topography, and natural resources. Thus, with their sails extended to the wind; the British ensign waiving and the national motto of *For God and my Right* pressed upon their lips, they charted a course to distant shores. It was a fateful journey that in due time changed world history.

# UNDOING OF AN EMPIRE

Initially, the purpose of exploration was to find faster trade routes to expand the trade in goods. However, by the 17th Century, international trade had taken on new meaning with an exotic commodity i.e., humans.

By the time British ships reached the shores of West Africa, the slave trade was already underway. European insertion was largely contained along the coastal regions so that the major cities of Timbuktu, Djenne and Gao, located thousands of miles away, went virtually untouched. Yet internal struggles within the West African Empire had wasted away much of its territory. Still, rulers rested on the assurance that the empire had never underwent a major attack from outside invaders; and, even though regions along the coastline had been breached, its Saharan border remained intact, keeping foreign armies at bay. So as slavery rattled the western coast, people living within the empire went about their lives, out of reach of Trans-Atlantic trade. Still, the empire's wealth in gold and other resources made them a continual target; and, among their more persistent adversaries were the Moors whose army had attempted several times to reach the Saharan border but failed. Moor warriors were experts with the scimitar sword and other weaponry. They were also highly skilled horsemen. Their sheik-style of dress included a turban-wrap for the head and a flowing burnoose worn as a cloak.

In their last attempt, the Moor army finally succeeded. This time they were led by El Mansur and Saharan traders that knew how to evade the desert perils. Upon reaching the city of Timbuktu, they caught the people unawares and with European firepower in hand, they easily defeated the West African army. Outwardly, the Moors looked a lot like the inhabitants for they too were a dark people with Arab and African descent. Their religion was also Islam. This however was the extent of their likeness for under Moorish rule the land became restive. In the truest sense, West Africa had entered its own "dark ages."

*"The Songhay [West African] empire at the end of the sixteenth century had become fatally content to exist upon the traditions of its former greatness...the Tarikk says, in words which might have applied to decadent Rome: "things continued thus, until towards the moment in which the Songhay [West African] dynasty approached its end and its empire ceased to exist. At this moment faith was exchanged for infidelity; there was nothing forbidden by God which was not openly done...because of these*

*abominations the Almighty in His vengeance drew down upon the Songhay [West African empire] the victorious army of the Moors"* – Flora Shaw, Author, *A Tropical Dependency*

# Chapter V

# The Pupil

# A NEW LAND

In a letter to Roger C. Weightman (Mayor of Washington) and less than two weeks before his death on July 4, 1826 (Independence Day) Thomas Jefferson wrote, **"All eyes are opened or are opening to the rights of man."**

Foregoing old fidelities to a mother country, they washed upon the barren shores of a new land. Some came with hopes of finding liberty, desirous of an egalitarian society, which had been so elusive in their former land. Others came with dreams of prosperity. All saw America as a kind of promise land. The journey from Europe by sea tested their endurance, but they risked it all for a brand new start.

With wide-open spaces and an abundance of greenery, this new land felt like paradise, in stark contrast to the bustling crowds in England. Yet they were ill-fitted for their new environment and many grew sick or died. Still more came, replenishing those who were lost. Their survival depended upon diplomacy and reliance upon Native American Indians who essentially saved their lives. In return, settlers would drive them from their land, even to the edge of extinction.

# THE VOYAGE

Soon after the first English colonies formed, slave ships docked at the Virginia port and within the bowel of each ship were African men, women and children whisked away from loved ones from fields by day and homes by night. Loaded aboard ships, they were hastened from the palm-lined coasts of Ouidah, Badagry and Goree Island; never to see Africa again. During their arduous six-week journey, the tearful guttural sounds of women and children filled the hull of the ship. Their voices scaled the walls, reverberating against wooden beams, seeping into the nooks and crannies. At times their cries were rhythmic, as if enmeshed with the sound of the waves that beat against the keel like a foreboding overture of things to come.

Wanting to gain the highest profits, British trading companies loaded slave vessels pound for pound to capacity so that people appeared like an agglomeration of parts crammed into the smallest space available. Typically, they lived in a space that was no bigger than six feet by one foot, smaller than the average coffin. They lay stacked on top of each other like shelves on a bookcase. Chains shackled their hands and feet with ringbolts linking them together. The confined space lent itself to sickness and along with exposure to European diseases hundreds of thousands if not more died. But Africa had ample supply. Some elected suicide over bondage and revolt was always imminent so that British soldiers and crew stayed readied with firearms. Slave trading companies with ships thoughtfully named *Grace of God* and *Hope*, transported millions of African people as slaves to the new world. The British Royal Trading Company alone was responsible for enslaving over two million African people.

# THE ARRIVAL

As each ship arrived at port, the *welcome wagon* consisted of a loud creaking door swinging open revealing a cargo of human ebony. Lying compact for much of the journey, an arabesque design of body parts unfolded. They represented various tribal communities with different cultures and languages.

Some of the many languages spoken were Ewe, Fante, Dugabi, Sohghai, Asante, Fular, Bambara, Wolof, Jola, Fon, Yoruba, Temne, Mende, Fulani, Hausa and Djernia. Each group was as distinct as any group of people or society could be; but what brought them all together, was something, which had never mattered in their homeland. Skin color. As they were led off the ship, their hearts were instantly stirred by the familiarities of home. A lapis azure sky, the bright sunshine and a slight breeze that skirted across their faces. But the moment was short lived; interrupted by the clanging of chains that bound their hands, neck, and feet. They had entered a strange land inhabited by what they believed were a horde of bad spirits. A land filled with brutal people. No doubt, slave traders saw Africans as strange as well for in their society, darkness equated something evil.

# AUCTIONEER'S BENCH

Little time was lent for acclimation as the business of buying and selling humans was brisk and unyielding. It happened during the course of a normal day. Men loaded up their wagons with supplies while women and children hurried along the promenade to the corner store. It was a scene that could have very well been taken from a Norman Rockwell painting if not for the human auction taking place in the center of town. Curious onlookers stood on the courthouse lawn as each person was led to the auctioneer's bench and then the bidding commenced. Slave brokers bought and sold people with the greatest of ease, as though bargaining for an ox or sound steed. While awaiting the swift pond of the gavel, they remained stoic, eyes void of compassion and at the final thud, a human life passed from freedom to slavery, forever. With cold-hearted indifference, they separated family members; husbands from wives, mothers from children and siblings alike.

*"We were not many days in the merchant's custody before we were sold...In this manner, without scruple, are relations and friends separated, most of them never to see*

*each other again... there were several brothers, who, in the sale, were sold in different lots; and it was very moving on this occasion to see and hear their cries at parting. "* -
Olaudah Equiano (African Prince and freed slave), *The Interesting Narrative, and Other Writings*, 1789

# FRUITFUL COMMERCE

Within a century of involvement in the slave trade, the British had once again stampeded over their competition. To secure their place at the top, the British entered into an agreement with Spain called the Asiento Treaty, whereby they promised to deliver at least 144,000 Africans to the Americas and Caribbean Islands within a three-year period. This lucrative agreement was over and above the number of slaves that the British were already transporting. It allowed them to monopolize the slave trade, which resulted in a feverish competition between participating nations.

As the number of colonies grew in America, so too would plantation farms spread throughout the south, so that the demand for agrarian slave labor also increased. At the time, owning slaves was acceptable in our society, mainly because of the mutual relationship between the institution of slavery and the fundamental success of the nation. Free labor quickly made plantation owners rich and the more money they made the more attached they became to the peculiar institution. The system of slavery in America would ultimately grow to rival that of ancient

Rome in both methodology and cruelty. At its peak, the number of slaves in America would exceed that of the Roman Empire. This is America's legacy.

# THE COMMONWEALTH

Steadily, America was building an economy based on agrarian slave labor. In areas where the climate was good and the soil was rich, lucrative crops like tobacco, indigo, rice and cotton were grown. In the low-countries of North and South Carolina, rice was copiously planted along tidal rivers and yielded the best profit. Sounds of calling marsh wrens, croaking frog, and chirping crickets lent a feeling of serenity to this environment. Oftentimes, calm waters were disrupted by mud puppies scampering across the tidewaters to a refuge beneath the riverbank. All of this tranquility gave no indication of the backbreaking work or the hostile environment that slaves had to endure. A day's requirement averaged around five-hundred pounds of rice – a strenuous goal. What's more, lurking beneath the murky waters were poisonous moccasins and deadly alligators. Not to mention it was a breeding ground for disease.

In Virginia, rows and rows of tobacco plants aligned thousands of acres of farmland and there was always a tinge of sweet tobacco in the air. Slaves spent a great deal of time chopping and processing tobacco, oftentimes well into the night.

In Georgia, cotton was king. To the nation, cotton was *white* gold. Because there was little waste in processing cotton, the profits were very high. And there was a huge demand for its choice fibers in factories in England and other parts of Europe where cotton was quickly replacing uncomfortable wool garments. But cotton was also labor-intensive, which meant that wealth in the south was contingent upon keeping slavery going.

In the summertime when the cotton was high and covered the fields like clouds coming to rest on earth, the time for picking was nigh. Field slaves whether men, women or children, labored for long stretches; some ten, twelve and fifteen hour days. While they labored, the sun basted their bodies until sweat broke through the skin to keep them from over-heating. A workday easily ran into night for after collecting, time had to be spent culling the white fibers by removing seeds and other debris. The daily quota for male slaves was around five-hundred pounds and for females, one-hundred pounds. Since half the weight of the cotton boll is in the seed, having to meet such large quotas took a great deal of time and energy so that little time was left for personal care. As a result, the steady plucking of the thorny bolls etched in their hands permanent scarring. The repetition made them claw-like and arthritic. The rest of the body wore down quickly.

Slaveholders were careful to remove Africans from regions already known for growing the crops they were interested in planting. Carolina planters wanted slaves from Sierra Leone or Ghana where they commonly grew rice. The people of Gambia, known for their physical strength, were desirable to cotton planters in Georgia. People in regions where indigo, flax, and tobacco were grown, caught the interest of Virginia planters. The profits gained from all of these crops, made the south unbelievably, rich and southern planters became the *fat cats* within society. The South grew to be the wealthiest region in the nation.

# INNOCENT AGE

Large antebellum homes dotted the southern landscape. Both in style and grandeur these plantations were reminiscent of noble estates in Europe, which was not by accident. Owners sent for pattern books from Europe and hired European architects to design special elements for their homes. These large-scale plantations stood as centerpieces in the land. Adorning the frontispiece were Greek columns and a porch that extended from one end of the home to the other. Seated on the porch were country style rockers where family and friends relaxed while sipping juleps on a hot sultry day. Inside there was a grand foyer with a side-parlor for guests and a meandering staircase, leading to the upstairs living quarters. Plantation owners spared no expense in decorating their home in lavish drapery, bedding and furniture. Outside, there was a beautifully landscaped garden with ornamental crepe myrtle and bull bay magnolia. Scents of camellia and honey-suckle lent a wonderful fragrance to the surroundings; and, at the slightest breeze hundreds of dandelion plumes took flight bouncing about the air like small crafts on bumpy seas. Homes were the hallmark of fine living and a testament of wealth. However, nothing was more impressive or symbolized high social standing than a healthy stock of slaves. The more you owned, the higher your social status was in the community. Another benefit from owning a large number of slaves was no labor costs. As such, wealth in the South flowed rather freely allowing them to indulge every whim imaginable. The English were finally able to live lifestyles comparable to the wealthiest in ancient Rome.

The wives of plantation owners devoted their time to personal fulfillment. They enjoyed building a culture based on romantic charm and intellectual posturing. Even more, they wanted to create a social persona befitting their status. Much of their time was spent on fabrications of all sorts. They paid great attention to their appearance and excitedly awaited the arrival of new fabrics. Silks and velvet imports were quite expensive and thus, used sparingly, as an accent on a coat or dress. Their southern sensibilities called for wholesome apparel with a feminine flair. They wore pannier puffs about the hips and a large bustle, which gave volume to the backside. A drawn corset flattered the waistline. Other popular accessories were the bell hoop and petticoat worn underneath mounds of skirt fabric. A head bonnet and gloves signified proper etiquette. Southern men were just as attentive to their appearance. They wore fashionable knee breeches and white shirts made of *lawn* fabric. There was *ruching* on the cuffs and the collar was decorated with *birds-crop* ruffles that also ran down the front of the shirt. A coat and gloves were part of the formalities of dress as well as a hat to adorn the head, which they respectfully removed in the presence of a woman.

The southern style of living was an attempt to create a utopia. They wanted to reap the wonderful benefits of the peculiar institution while dismissing the harsh realities of slavery. This meant that their acute disregard for the damage they were doing was deliberate. The wives of slave masters lent a certain refinement to this blissful ignorance. Relishing in their own newfound freedoms and authority they neatly tucked away the horrors of slavery. And with their words, they encouraged husbands in the role of slave master, making sure that it fit them well like a fine redingote coat. But refusing to acknowledge the horrors of slavery could not remove the effects. Even more, slavery stood in direct opposition of freedom and democracy, prescribed by the forefathers of this nation. But this truth was an even weightier matter for these men as both George Washington and Thomas Jefferson, among others, owned a large number of slaves. This tells us that the most basic attributes of freedom had not been fully realized, even by the founding fathers. Most assuredly,

America as a young democracy founded upon freedom and liberty, was still a work in progress.

# RACHEL WEEPS

The role of a female house-slave varied from laboring in the master's household to providing hands-on care for his children even to the neglect of her own. The master was amenable to her motherly instincts and therefore held no inhibitions about placing his child into her care. Ultimately, a natural bond developed between child and slave, which grew even more when she was asked to lend her lactating breast when the wife was unable to produce milk. Her life was filled with endless responsibilities but little reward. She found a semblance of fulfillment when in secret she married and formed a family of her own away from the prying eyes of the master. She juggled the care of both families preparing quality meals for the master's family while making do with what was considered as inedible foods for her own. Generations of healthy eating by ancestors had made Africans physically strong but good nutrition in this new land had worked against them. Seemingly, this legacy made them more capable of enduring the harshness of slavery more so than the European indigent or the American Indian. But in America, their diets had drastically changed for the worse for the main food they now ate was pig and not the choicest parts either but the throwaways - the hocks, ears, hooves, intestines and skin. Remarkably out of these discards, she created delicacies. When available she added familiar staples such as greens, ground mills, and yams. In this way, she preserved the generations.

In the days of Roman slavery, a child born to a female slave was automatically the property of the master. America's institution of slavery applied the same law. This meant that the offspring of slaves was the property of the plantation owner, to do with whatever he pleased. It was the most heart-wrenching aspect of the peculiar institution. For in an instant, the child of slaves could be sold off to another plantation. As a result, countless children would never feel their mother's embrace or sit upon her warm lap and lean against her soft breast. They would never hear the whisper of her voice or feel their heart flicker at the sight of her welcoming smile. In every significant way it was "Rachel weeping for her children, and would not be comforted, because they are not" (Matthew 2:18).

The children were lost forever.

How a slaveholder handled the offspring of a female slave depended upon whether or not it benefitted him. He allowed the mother to keep her child if she could instill an acceptance for their lot in life. He preferred that rather than having to break-in a new slave that was oftentimes contumacious against being enslaved. But if he found that it was more profitable to sell the child, he would do so without hesitation. In this way, he routinely interrupted the connection between mother and child, leaving a scar too deep to repair.

*"I never saw my mother to know her as such, more than four or five times in my life; and each of these times was very short in duration and, at night... She made her journeys to see me at night traveling the whole distance on foot, after the performance of her day's work. She was a field hand and a whipping is the penalty of not being in the field at sunrise...I do not recollect of ever seeing my mother by the light of day. She was with me in the night. She would lie down with me and get me to sleep, but long before I waked, she was gone. Very little communication ever took place between us."* – Frederick Douglass, Freed Slave

If a mother was allowed to rear her child, she did so under the strict and watchful eye of the peculiar institution. In this environment, she exchanged her motherly tendencies, for repression. Knowing that the master made sharp contrasts between his world and that of a slave, she raised them *not* to have a want for success. In order to preserve her child's life, she quenched their hopes and dreams of having anything more than their current state. Her guarded love protected them from a harsher penalty.

*"For what this separation has done, I do not know, unless it be to hinder the development of the child's affection towards its mother, to blunt and destroy the natural affection of the mother for the child. This is the inevitable result"*- Frederick Douglass, Freed Slave

# PLAGUE OF THE HEART

Marriage between slaves was illegal, making procreation a matter of breeding. Other laws prohibited slaves from getting a formal education and it was illegal for them to read or write. In fact, they could not show any interest in the culture in which they lived, leaving the extent of their learning limited to the needs of the slave owner. Over the course of time such mandates all but destroyed the ancestral building blocks of family and community. Disconnected from their history, memories of Africa began to fade away, along with the roles of mother, father, and child. With coarse hands they had sewn into the soil and the earth had given of its bounty but yet, they could no more reap the benefits or call themselves American than the draft animals that plowed the fields. Culture, family, and community were gone. An intentional act. To strip them of everything so that the only thing left to cling to was their intimacy with slavery.

*"She [mother] died when I was about seven years old...I was not allowed to be present during her illness, at her death or burial: she was gone long before I knew anything about it. Never having enjoyed to any considerable*

*extent, her soothing presence, her tender and watchful care, I received the tiding of her death with much the same emotions I should have probably felt at the death of a stranger"-* Frederick Douglass, Freed Slave, Orator, Abolitionist

They were marked by an *inescapable* blackness. In Africa, melanin cells darkened their skin, saving them from deadly ultraviolet rays from the sun. But in this new world dark skin represented something wrong or inferior so that the abiding ethos was one of self-hate. However, there was always calm resistance. Many relied upon the dictates of grandsires speaking out from distant shores. It was the voices of the elders, beckoning them to hold on to ancestral memories of family and community. "God's arm never waivers," they said, "So put your trust in Him." In regards to their plight, the elders said, "The hunger that has hope for its satisfaction, does not kill." Proverbs like these helped them to hold fast to hope while urging them not to hate. Like sacred passages, they passed these teachings along to their children and to the generations.

## YEARNING FOR FREEDOM

"If you want to speak to God, tell it to the wind," said the grandsires. So they did, in song. While laboring, they sang about their condition and God's deliverance so that fields became their chapels.

*"Go down Moses, 'Way down in Egypt land, tell ole Pharaoh, and let my people go."* American Negro Spiritual

Although within earshot, slaveholders dismissed slave songs as crude colloquialisms having no meaning at all. But "A deaf ear is followed by death and an ear that listens, is followed by blessings." Sage words from the elders. Without a doubt, their songs had purpose. Songs that were spiritual intended to break through the firmament and reach the throne of God. Songs that were about freedom, brought the many cultures and languages together in one consensus, unifying them under the cause of freedom.

*"O freedom, O freedom, O freedom over me. An' befo' I'd be a slave, I'll be buried in my grave. An' go home to my Lord an' be free."* - Negro Spiritual

At the end of the day, the slaves welcomed the night when the moon replaced the sun and stars scintillated against the blackened sky. As darkness drew near, the soft rumblings of their voices continued to pierce the silence. Like the voices of African Griots, the songs carried to distances far away taking them beyond their physical constraints. Their songs of importunity toward God were unyielding and yet, each day validated their condition as slaves. The long permanence of their circumstances made their pleas seem futile but renewed hope came with the dawning of a new day. Their understanding of one God had transformed into an acceptance of Jesus Christ and Christianity. They readily took hold of the universal message of love spoken by Jesus. However, what they did not accept was the kind of Christianity extolled by many whites that condoned slavery. Out of all of the White Christian groups, only one actively resisted slavery. The Society of Friends, the Quakers, spoke out publicly against slavery, calling it sin.

# THE FAVOR OF GOD

A slave nation that is simultaneously a Christian nation. These two institutions do not agree. To align slavery with the Christian message, members of the clergy created new interpretations of Bible scripture and then went about the land spreading the virtues of slavery from south of the Mason Dixon and beyond.

*"I daily perceive that many things are done here out of a worldly and [self] interested principle, and little for God's sake"-* Frances Le Jau of St. Paul's Parish in S. Carolina 1709

Sounds of Sunday morning. Of cantering horses and creaking wagon wheels; the muffled pounding of feet moving down the dirt path. It was time for church. Compared to the grand styles of European monasteries, the Southern Protestant Church was of simple construction, built with basic masonry materials, whitewashed walls and the familiar steeple on top. Inside this modest building was a main sanctuary with rows of wooden pews. At the front of the room stood a wooden lectern raised slightly higher than the pews, serving as the pulpit. Here, the minister preached sermons about heaven and hell. He prescribed God's favor to the white race but to the black race, he assigned His curse. A curse, which had taken place over seven-thousand years earlier and supposedly, left black people in a perpetual state of affliction with slavery as a result. Yet the curse they referred to was actually wrought by Noah and not by God but irrespective to that, why would a curse occurring so long ago, still be relevant? Where was the mercy of God in that narrative?

*"I rose at 5 o' clock this morning and read a chapter in Hebrew and 200 verses in Homer's Odyssey. I ate milk for breakfast. I said my prayers. Jenny and Eugene were whipped. I danced my dance."* — William Byrd, Slave Owner, *The Secret Diaries of William Byrd 1709-1712*

Nevertheless, this explanation of a curse satisfied white churchgoers. It spared slaveholders from judgment and caste more blame on the already impoverished souls of slaves. But slaves would question a color-struck God.

*"...I love the pure, peaceable and impartial Christianity of Christ; I therefore hate the corrupt, slaveholding, women-whipping, cradle-plundering, partial and hypocritical Christianity of this land"..."The man who wields the blood-clotted cow skin during the week fill the pulpit on Sunday and claims to be a minister of the meek and lowly Jesus"* — Frederick Douglass, Freed Slave, Orator, Abolitionist 1845

# FASHIONED IDEATIONS

It is clear that the institution of slavery brought tremendous wealth to America, which was largely contained in the south. With wealth came influence and leaders in the South used their power to rally support for slavery. Not just for slavery to continue but also for it to expand into new territories.

To ensure long lasting support for slavery newspapers, periodicals and books were filled with negative imagery portraying blacks as lawless, amoral and savage. Illustrations depicted them as ape-like with bulging eyes and lagging big lips, making them appear less human. This propaganda spread across America. The heaviest distribution was in the South where people were inundated by these materials, as though lessoning the barrage would break the spell. Such imagery along with church inculcations painted a very scary picture. Support for these ideas also came from academia— particularly studies related to science and philosophy. All of this information would build up animosity toward slaves and a lack of affinity for their plight. Though fiercely promoted in America, these ideas began in

England and Western Europe. America was merely the pupil as England was the teacher.

# AGE OF SCIENCE

In the early days, what was coined as *science* often lacked pure scientific method, which involves theory, controlled experimentation and observation as well as trials and measurements. In addition, there is proper debate and an alternative theory. Without these mechanisms in place, there is lots of room for error. During this time of scientific growth, one of the more popular scientists of the era was the Englishman Charles Darwin, born in England, the same day as Lincoln, February 12, 1809. Religion was introduced in both of these men's lives at an early age but as an adult, Darwin denied God's existence.

*"There is no evidence that man was aboriginally endowed with the ennobling belief in the existence of an Omnipotent God"* – Charles Darwin, *The Descent of Man*, 1871

His atheism also weighed heavily upon his scientific studies.

*"The universe we observe has precisely, the properties we should expect if there is, at bottom, no design, no purpose, no evil, no good, nothing but blind pitiless*

*indifference"* – Charles Darwin, *On the Origin of Species,* 1859

In contrast, Abraham Lincoln acknowledged his Christian upbringing throughout his adult life.

*"...In regards to this Great Book [Bible], I have but to say, it is the best gift God has given to man."* – Abraham Lincoln, 16th President, 1864

But similarities in birth and upbringing did not translate into adulthood in matters of race. Darwin believed in the subjugation of what he called the "lower races" or people of color.

*"But the inheritance of property by itself is very far from an evil...and it is chiefly through their power that the civilized [white] races have extended, and are now everywhere extending their range, so as to take the place of the lower races."* — Charles Darwin, *The Descent of Man,* 1871

Abraham Lincoln expressed a very different view.

*"As I would not be a slave, so I would not be a master. This expresses my idea of democracy. Whatever differs from this, to the extent of the difference, is no democracy"* — Abraham Lincoln, 1858

Both would go on to play critical roles in the matter of race within their own nations and throughout the world but for completely opposite reasons. The actions of one would be to the detriment of an entire race of people and the actions of the other would be to the benefit of that same race.

# RE-CREATION OF MAN

A love of natural science persuaded Darwin to go on a five-year excursion, traveling on a ship called "The Beagle." During his travels to remote lands, he chronicled his observations of native animals and plants. Based on this extensive work, Darwin wrote a book called *On the Origin of Species by Means of Natural Selection, or the Preservation of Favored Races in the Struggle for Life.* Information contained within this book was considered groundbreaking, so much so, that within a matter of days it completely sold out in Western Europe and America. It was a prelude to his next book published years later called *The Descent of Man.* In this second book, Darwin applied some of his previous discoveries on the evolution of animals, to humans. More specifically, Darwin developed a theory that determined humans evolved from the ape. His theory astounded the western world for as far back as human accounts bear out and no matter what culture, people have believed in Divine creation. Now, according to Darwin, man was not created in the image of God but rather in the image of an ape. His evolutionary design included placing humans into categories based on skin color and other physical traits. Darwin determined that Africans, especially those with the darkest skin-color, were a sub-species of human. An intermediate man. The break between a fully- evolved white man and the ape. This led Darwin to assume that intelligence and moral capabilities were decided by race as well. For that reason, he placed the white race at the "summit" of human intelligence and moral capacity and at the bottom were darker skinned people, having the lowest intelligence and moral capability. In the area of intelligence, Darwin surmised that blacks were incapable of reaching the same level of intelligence as whites. And in the area of moral capacity, he decided that blacks were amoral and thus unable to tell the difference between right and wrong. Furthermore, he said that blacks could neither understand nor reciprocate "complex emotions" such as love and compassion.

In support of his racial science, Darwin compared the sloping skull, dark skin (face, feet, hands) and other features of black people with the gorilla. By this comparison, Darwin concluded that black people were closest to the gorilla and chimpanzee making them neither fully ape nor completely human. This basically summed up his proof in support of his racial theories. What was glaringly missing from Darwin's theory however, was that Europeans as well as other people around the world, share the same skull shape as the great apes. Decidedly, humans have a similar skull shape to other primates regardless of where they are from, not just black people as Darwin suggested. True science recognizes this fact. Another observation used by Darwin was the skin color of apes vs. black people. Here again, he ignored the fact that the skin color of many types of apes is actually *pale whitish* and not black. Nevertheless, ideas like these were popular in those days, surfacing anytime a society needed to rationalize harming another group of people. Still, Darwin's ideas were unique for he had added the credibility of science to authenticate his racial theories. This also made his ideas more dangerous.

Obviously, social influences skewed Darwin's ideals on race; for, he lived during a time when imperialism dominated the national policy. A time of taking control over weaker lands and subjugating the people under English authority and will. Having placed his race at the top of the evolutionary ladder, Darwin determined that this position of hierarchy was fixed. Their spot at the top could *never* be altered or surpassed by any other race. His race science took on a sinister tone when he claimed that the darker races would ultimately be brought to extinction by the white race.

*"The partial or complete extinction of many races of man is historically known... When civilized [white] nations*

*come in contact with barbarians [dark races] the struggle is short..."* Charles Darwin, *The Descent of Man*, 1871

In order to maintain a racial hierarchy Darwin would turn on his own. Those who he believed degraded the white race such as the weak, sickly, handicapped, and mentally unstable. He suggested that they not be allowed to bear children or to marry. He even surmised that their medical help be withheld. In doing so, he sought to *purify* the white race.

*"...Thus the weak members of civilized societies propagate their kind. No one who has attended to the breeding of domestic animals will doubt that this must be highly, injurious to the race of man. It is surprising how soon a want of care or care wrongly, directed, leads to the degeneration of a domestic race..."* - Charles Darwin, *The Descent of Man, 1871*

To be sure, Darwin's racial theories fit well within the times in which he lived and overtime he would grow in recognition, his fame spreading throughout the Western world; and yet, the voice of resistance could still be heard.

*"This charge of inferiority is an old dodge. It has been made available for oppression on many occasions. It is only about six centuries since the blue-eyed and fair-haired Anglo-Saxons were considered inferior by the haughty Normans who once trampled upon them. If you*

*read the history of the Norman Conquest, you will find that this proud Anglo-Saxon was looked upon as a coarser clay than his Norman master and might be found in the highways and byways of Old England laboring with a brass collar on his neck and the [brand] of his master marked upon it.*" —Frederick Douglass, Freed Slave, Orator, Abolitionist

# A GREAT DECEPTION

"It is easy to lie about a distant place," the elders would say. A fitting proverb for what had taken place with the British over the last few centuries. So far removed from their time of servitude they now claimed themselves a superior breed. If the British were truly interested in pure science then it would have been easy to disprove claims of superior and inferior races. For in America freed slaves had become educated orators, editors, inventors and businessmen putting to rest the idea that intelligence was isolated to whites alone. Furthermore, it had not taken them an evolutionary span to reach these academic levels but rather a matter of decades. Even more to their credit, they made these accomplishments along the periphery of a society marked by racism and thus, inherently resistant to their success. This would *fly in the face* of what Darwin would later surmise. For by his estimations it should have taken them thousands or even hundreds of thousands of years to evolve to such a level. Too long to have taken place within a human lifetime. At the very least, their successes should have offered an alternative to Darwin's ideas for their activities were not done beneath a rock and some were published for the world to see.

# TAKING FLIGHT

Racial ideas that developed in Western Europe served to support the institution of slavery in America. Racial science so convoluted the issue of slavery, it made it difficult to criticize the institution. But slaves grew tired of a want for freedom and their best option for now was to flee.

A slave caught in the act of escape was severely punished. The method of chastising came from the end of a six-foot long bullwhip loaded at the tip with buckshot for effectiveness. The event was made into a big affair by the overseer for everyone was expected to attend in order to witness the beating of a neighbor or family member. Hands were tied to the whipping post and clothes were stripped to expose the back. Then the bullwhip was duly applied, peeling away the skin like a ripened melon. These public displays were intended to horrify slaves and to act as a deterrent for others from having the same urges. Yet a want for freedom could no more be beaten out of them than any other natural desire. Gathering up the broken body they attended to the wounds with healing salve from the tree of

Bethlehem.

*"In every human breast, God has implanted a principle which we call love of freedom, it is impatient of oppression and pants for deliverance... I will assert that same principle lives in us. God grant Deliverance..."* –
Phyllis Wheatley, 1774

And still they ran. Leaving behind life as a slave in much the same way as they were stolen. By night, in secret and in haste. Their way of escape was aided by a communication network that quietly navigated from one state to the next.

*"The Negroes have a wonderful art of communicating intelligence among themselves; it will run several hundreds of miles in a week or fortnight"* –John Quincy Adams, 6th U.S. President (Personal diary excerpt, conversation with Archibald Bulloch and John Houston southern delegates) 1831

The path to freedom was sewn on heirloom quilts that hung on the back porch. Within the morass of broken expression in song, there were cryptic messages. Ways of escape and wishes for Godspeed.

Pure arrogance kept slaveholders from seeing what was happening in plain sight. To them an ignorant slave could never circumvent the obstacles they had in place. But slaves continued to take flight and each successful escape motivated another. In an effort to curtail the number of escapees, slaveholders tightened their restrictions on slaves and increased runaway patrols. The world of a slave was made even smaller causing a pressure cooker effect that at times boiled over into insurrection.

*"When you make men slaves...you compel them to live with you in a state of war"* — Olaudah Equiano (African Prince and freed slave), *The Interesting Narrative, and Other Writings*, 1789

As more slaves escaped to freedom, leaders in southern states pushed for stronger laws that allowed them to pursue and recover runaways into Free States. However, slaves just kept on running, undeterred by these laws, for the ballast weighed heaviest on the side of freedom.

# ART OF ESCAPE

The South had all the power of the law on their side. Considering all they were up against, what then could a slave do? Clearly, escaping was not done on impulse for if re-captured, life became harder to bear. Much hope for a safe passage rested upon Divine intervention. God's heavenly compass that shone bright like an ornament in the sky – the North Star or what African elders called the *drinking gourd* would guide them to freedom. If a slave made it to the first checkpoint, a scout awaited to take him or her further north. Among the scouts, there was one name whispered along underground routes more than any other. Harriet Tubman. She was a slight woman, appearing older than her rightful age. Maybe because her body preserved the scars of slavery. She was an unlikely liberator but highly successful at leading slaves to freedom. To slaves located along the eastern coast of Maryland, she was a savior. After bravely executing her own escape she made many trips back repeatedly risking her freedom to guide family and others north as far as Canada. Her movements were so secretive, no one really knows how many slaves Harriet actually helped but if the bounty of forty thousand dollars, which is equivalent to one million dollars today, is any indication then Harriet was a very serious threat. She made known to all that her belief in God guided her steps.

*" [I] have never met with any person [like Harriet Tubman] of any color who had more confidence in the voice of God, as spoken direct to her soul…and her faith in a Supreme Power was great"* – Thomas Garret, Quaker, 1860

With her small convoy of runaways, Harriet traveled hundreds of miles north along riverbanks and Appalachian terrain. Once the decision to escape was made there was no turning back for Harriet branded a pistol to turn aside a fleeting heart. Much aid for runaways came from both black and white sympathizers. She relied upon Quakers who risked their lives to help, as a duty to God, they said.

*"Quakers almost as good as colored….They call themselves friends and you can trust them every time"* – Harriet Tubman, 1849

Reaching the end of their journey, life as a slave shed away like the removal of grave clothes. They were free.

*"I looked at my hands, to see if I was the same person now that I was free. There was such a glory over everything; the sun came like gold through the trees, and*

*over de fields, and I felt like I was in heaven."* – Harriet
Tubman, 1849

To Harriet and the others, freedom was sufficient for
"The bitter heart eats its owner," so said the elders.
Thus, they did not take revenge upon those who had
mistreated them. The number of slaves that escaped is
not known but most assuredly, each departure left a
chink in the wall of the peculiar institution.

# ANOTHER WAY OUT

Besides escape, another way to freedom was to buy your way out. Most often, males did so, but it was no easy task. When time was allotted, they earned money by working odd jobs such as blacksmithing. The process could take years but after building up a reserve and with the agreement of the owner, he bought his freedom.   If possible, he also bought the freedom of his son rather than a wife or a daughter for he knew all too well, how contrary slavery was to the natural condition of a man even more so than to a woman. A son could also help earn money so that the whole family could be redeemed.

# FREEDOM MOVEMENT

If we consider all that slaves were doing to resist their condition, no doubt slaves themselves caused the institution to falter. There were uprisings but it was rare. Although they knew where the ammunition houses that stored the guns were located, most of them did not choose revolt. The answer to freedom was by non-violent means.

Outside the institution, more and more people were calling for the demise of slavery. Freed men and women as well as whites and some in the South were speaking out about the injustices of slavery. This was the first freedom movement in America. It forced the nation to remove the blinders and fairly examine the moral wrongs of slavery. America now faced a marvelous conundrum. The time was at hand when the nation could no longer vacillate between two opinions.

The genesis of this freedom movement began about a half century earlier during the time of the War of Independence. It was a movement not waged by bloodshed or bullets but by an appeal to the highest moral right. In letters sent to Congress both slave and freed men petitioned leaders to free the slaves and to give blacks the same rights as whites. Their ardent appeal was based on the same principles of freedom in which the nation had fought for in the War of Independence. They further contended that the U.S. Constitution made no mention of race or skin color when defining citizenship. Therefore, the millions of blacks born on American soil must be considered as citizens. Now, decades later, abolitionists were once again using the U.S. Constitution and Declaration of Independence to reveal blatant contradictions in matters of freedom and justice.

*"We hold these truths to be self-evident that all men are created equal, that they are endowed by their Creator with certain unalienable Rights, that among these are Life, Liberty and the pursuit of Happiness"* –United States of America, Declaration of Independence

As slavery became more engrained in the South, England and other western lands made slavery illegal. Now the world watched as America worked out its duel nature: That of being a Christian nation while holding one eighth of the population in captivity and that of a democracy while condoning legalized slavery.

# QUESTION OF LIBERTY

The want for freedom by slaves. The want for slavery to continue by southerners. Both boiled down to necessity. However, times were changing. In the North, the economy was transitioning into industry but in the South, the economy continued to be driven by agriculture with slavery at the core. And yet, the South had one advantage. Cotton. Still king, the demand for cotton continued to increase so that for a while at least, slavery had to relent to financial gain. But the matter persisted.

*"... That [slavery] is the root of almost all the troubles of the present and the fears for the future"* – John Quincy Adams, 6th U.S. President, 1831

As the financial mainstay in the nation moved from agriculture to industry, the question of freedom once again pushed to the forefront. The activities of abolitionists within Free States in the North began to spread overseas causing more pressure on the U.S. government to end slavery. But any interference with slavery was looked upon by southerners as a threat to their livelihoods. They saw the institution of slavery as an important contributor to the nation's growth. For two centuries it was an acceptable part of society in the North as well as in the South and now northerners actively sought to end it. Their actions were viewed by southerners as hypocritical and they resented what they saw as meddling from outsiders. Now "The chickens had come home to roost." For a nation that builds upon the sufferings of others is never a moral good. Neither is it righteous. Yet the South was unwilling to change. They hated abolitionists and took great offense to their use of laws to further their cause. So in response, southern leaders used the same laws as had abolitionists but in *support* of slavery. They declared that the laws governing the land were intended to protect the rights and privileges of white citizens only and that the laws gave them the right to exert power in any way they saw fit including capturing and owning slaves. Taking a *laissez-faire* approach, they asserted that government had no business interfering in commercial affairs namely, their slave commerce. They further interpreted the laws as giving them the right to protect their livelihood by any necessary means. In essence, they had no problem demanding their own rights while prohibiting the rights of others.

# A WIDENING DIVIDE

The South was certainly on the defensive. Southern members of Congress began to obstruct the passing of laws and obscured the real issues concerning slavery.

*"...Nothing is better established than that a large black population cannot live among whites, except as servants, there is no other mode to make the blacks useful or tolerable or to prevent extermination. "* Harper's Weekly, African American History in The Press 1851-1899

Despite their attempts to conceal the truth, plenty of eyewitnesses to the cruelties of slavery would not be silenced.

*"...A mild affectionate and docile people. They have received from us who claim to be a superior race, a treatment which of itself disproves our superiority"* - Harper's Weekly, African American History in The Press 1851-1899

While southern leaders worked to keep the status quo, the federal government moved to contain the spread of slavery into new territories. The South saw these attempts as adversarial. More and more, opinions in the north were at odds with those in the South. As the divide widened a clash of titanic proportions seemed inevitable.

# CULTIVATING AN ADVERSARY

*By a wing and a prayer*, Abraham Lincoln was elected as the 16th President of the United States of America. His looming six-foot-three-inch frame lent itself to the noble figure he would become. He was rather thin in size with an octoroon complexion. During his childhood, he was immersed in the Quaker religion so that as an adult he adamantly opposed slavery. This made him an instant enemy of the South.

*"...If slavery is not wrong, nothing's wrong..."* – Abraham Lincoln, 16th U.S. President 1864

If there was a single incident which stands out as the trigger that changed this simmering dispute into out-and-out war, arguably, it was Lincoln's election as President. In less than two months after his election, South Carolina seceded from the Union. Within the next six months Mississippi, Florida, Alabama, Georgia, Louisiana, Texas, Virginia, Arkansas, Tennessee and North Carolina also seceded. Almost the entire south had broken away from the Union. Lincoln initially did nothing about this posturing until southern rebels seized the federal fort in Sumter. Raising the flag of the Confederacy, the South positioned itself as a separate nation. In response, Lincoln called for Federal forces to squelch the rebellion.

# WAR BETWEEN BROTHERS

Slaves called it the "Big Break Out."

The majority of civil war battles were concentrated in Virginia, the Carolinas, Tennessee and Georgia. In every significant way, the South was prepared for this war between patriot brothers. With the best military minds at their disposal along with the totality of their wealth, they were a formidable enemy. Early on, the major victories went to the Confederate soldiers, who showed no signs of relenting. The uncertainties of what this monumental dispute might mean to the Union, weighed heavily upon Lincoln. Nevertheless, he stayed the course, submitting to a higher source to determine what was ultimately, a moral dispute.

*"If God now wills the removal of a great wrong and wills also, that we of the North as well as you of the South, shall pay fairly, for our complicity in that wrong, impartial history will find therein new cause to attest and revere the justice and goodness of God"* – Abraham Lincoln, 16th U.S. President

For the next three years, the nation stood transfixed by this bloody encounter. Northern troops had not been successful at penetrating deep within rebel lines and the standoff had begun to take a toll on the North. At the urging of abolitionists, Lincoln finally allowed black men to enlist as soldiers in the Federal Army. Thus, they joined the battle, fighting valiantly on behalf of the Union and for freedom. Enlistments were very high. In Kentucky, a free southern state, black enlisters filled volumes of draft books. There was George Paris, age 22 from Georgia; Marshall McFerris, age 22 from Mississippi; Cecil Brown, 27; Jacob Cox, 22; Sidney Sanders, 24; Whitney Harrison, 29; Ruben Gibbs, 21; Ed Jenkins, 32; Miles Mays, 38; Moses Coleman, 24; Stephen McElroy, 21; Henry Craig, 20 and many more. These men were farmers, coopers, *sea-borers* and blacksmiths. They worked as teamsters driving horses to haul freight; colliers aboard coal ships; railroad porters and stablemen. They came to Kentucky from Massachusetts, North Carolina, South Carolina, New Orleans, Washington DC, Tennessee and New York. Their numbers grew to almost two hundred thousand soldiers.

*"And then, there will be some black men who can remember that, with silent tongue, and clenched teeth, and steady eye, and well-poised bayonet, they have helped mankind on to this great consummation..."* - Abraham Lincoln, 16th U.S. President

Conditions of service for black soldiers were marked by poor treatment. They received lower pay than their white counterparts as well as inadequate provisions. Still they fought with a valor unmatched by anyone for they were driven by an interminable desire to see the Union succeed.

*"You say you will not fight to free Negroes. Some of them are willing to fight for you..."* — Abraham Lincoln, 16th U.S. President

Black infantries were made up of bond and free as well as educated and uneducated. For all, the stakes were very high. The war symbolized the last great obstacle to freedom so they fought with a determination that embodied their battle cry to "Never Give Up!"

*"...Both in the South and in the North, they [blacks] are helping us – helping our soldiers that escape from rebel prisons, and going from our midst to help them fight our battles for us. Hunted to death by the mobs in our cities, they retaliate by joining our armies and they do their duty on the battlefield."* - Harper's Weekly, "African American History in The Press" 1851-1899

Some in the North opposed black soldiers in the Union army. As a result, these soldiers could never be assured that white soldiers would show them the same brotherhood in war as they showed each other. They fought anyway. Hatred for them in the South was palpable and black soldiers knew that if caught by the enemy, normal prisoner of war standards would not apply to them. Even so, they continued to fight and die.

*"...And then we saw the lightning and that was the guns; and then we heard the thunder and that was the big guns; and then we heard the rain falling and that was the drops of blood falling and when we came to get the crops, it was the dead that we reaped"* – Description of 54th. Massachusetts Black Regiment Battle at Fort Wagner by Harriet Tubman, Union Nurse

# MARCH TO THE SEA

Black reinforcements came at the gravest time of war, when Union casualties outnumbered Southern rebels and the victory tilted in favor of the Confederacy. Fierce battles between the North and the South continued until finally the tide began to turn. Union soldiers pressed against the rebel stronghold until they reached the red clay dirt of Georgia. Then they marched toward Atlanta, the heartbeat of the Confederacy.

The railway system in Atlanta was the center point in which ammunition and other vital supplies were delivered to the South. After arriving in Atlanta, Union soldiers destroyed the railway and burned down the city to its cinders, leaving piles of black ash to be scattered by the wind. This victory was the momentum they needed to push further south through Georgia. While marching, they destroyed canals and bridges, isolating Confederate brigades. With the exception of homes used as makeshift hospitals, they set afire every slaveholding plantation in their path, lighting up the land like a giant furnace. The plantation, which had been the symbol of the Grand Ole' South was utterly wiped away.

The music and gaiety was silenced. The lifestyle they so dearly loved and so desperately tried to hold on to had ended. Their worst fears had come upon them. How ironic that the demise of slavery had actually been orchestrated by the South for the Emancipation Proclamation never called for slavery to end. Neither had it freed *all* the slaves but only those living within rebel states. Thus it was their unyielding attachment to the peculiar institution, which had caused it to end. War had depleted most of the wealth gained through slavery, leaving the South bankrupt.

# A MORE PERFECT UNION

After four bloody years of civil eruption, the Southern Confederacy was defeated. The vestiges of war had left Old Glory tattered but our flag still waived with an even deeper relevance. The loss of life was far reaching for the blood tides washed over every American family. As many as a **half-million** people were dead. More people died in this single war than in all the American wars before or since combined. Yet even in the midst of such immense loss and still floundering in defeat, southerners remained unrepentant. What was more mind-boggling was that they saw themselves as the savior of black folk.

*"The idea that the Southern people are hostile to the Negroes, and would oppress them if it were in their power to do so, is entirely, unfounded. They have grown up in our midst, and we have been accustomed from childhood to look upon them with kindness."* – General Robert E. Lee, Harper's Weekly, African American History in The Press 1851-1899

Certainly, a handful of slaveholders treated their slaves with a measure of humanity but such behavior was hardly attributive to the majority. Still southerners commonly thought of slavery in this manner, which showed the depth of their emotional bluntness. Wild rationalizations like these bent them toward an even stronger delusion for many believed that manumitted slaves would rather stay in their *care* than be free. In this instance, a greater dose of reality was in order. As word of emancipation navigated through the North and down to the deepest parts of the South, *at one fell swoop,* they claimed their freedom. Their departure was as significant as the parting of the Red Sea and they never looked back.

Lincoln had triumphed in retaining the Union. He had realized the end of slavery but unfortunately his successes would conclude in the gravest personal sacrifice. In the aftermath of war, beneath the surface, bitter feelings were brewing against Lincoln. Mostly from southerners but bad sentiments also came from people in the North. No one who had benefited from slavery was happy. Lincoln had long since established his dislike for slavery but for centuries slavery served as the cornerstone of the society so that he also struggled with the right and wrongs of such matters.

*"...My paramount objective in this struggle is to save the Union, and is not either to save or to destroy slavery. If I could save the Union without freeing any slave I would do it and if I could save it by freeing all the slaves I would do it; and if I could save it by freeing some and leaving others alone I would also do that."*
- Abraham Lincoln, 16th U.S. President

Some whites branded him as a traitor to his race; sentiments that now seethed within the deepest recesses of the heart. Such an implication was a very dangerous matter and under these social pressures, Lincoln acquiesced. Freedom for slaves would not mean being truly free.

*"I will say then that I am not, nor ever have been in favor of bringing about in anyway the social and political equality of the white and black races...and I will say in addition to this that there is a physical difference between the white and black races which I believe will forever forbid the two races living together on terms of social and political equality."*- Abraham Lincoln, 16th U. S. President

Before completing the passing of the 13th Amendment, which made slavery illegal in all states, Lincoln was killed by a southern sympathizer. Yet his death would not turn back the clock. His efforts were very much alive and moving the nation toward change. Months after his death, the 13th Amendment would pass and become the law of the land. Southerners remained resistant to change and began to pass state laws that stunted the impact of the 13th Amendment. They put into place laws to hinder black people from receiving a good education, decent housing and making economic progress. Local Black Codes and Jim Crow laws restricted them from having full rights as citizens. There were also laws passed that effectively punished white people who crossed racial lines. White supremacy groups like the Klu Klux Klan received widespread membership from all sectors of society from teachers, business people, police, judges and at least one U.S. President. Thus, racism became acceptable in American society. As the rights of black citizens deteriorated, the nation stood silent. Many whites feared the negative social imprint they would suffer by speaking out or standing up for the rights of black people. And herein is the most glaring problem with racism as well as the notion of superior and inferior races; for, if indeed there was an actual *inferior race* then why the need to strewn obstacles across their path? Why hinder?

*"...You say, "what should we do with the black man"? If you will only untie his hands and give him a chance, I think he will live. He will work as readily for himself as the white man."*- Frederick Douglass, Freed Slave, Orator, Abolitionist

# ALLUSIVENESS OF EQUALITY

In the end, black Americans were forced to live outside of mainstream society making it necessary for them to build a society within a society. Words expressed within the Emancipation Proclamation and the 13th Amendment had given way to racial constructs that were too deeply embedded. A more potent unguent was needed to cure the ills of the nation. The way to healing began with forgiveness. Slavery had devastated families. Leaders of the institution had tried to destroy the humanity of blacks. Moreover, slavery served as a buttress for social racism. In light of all these things, one might think that every ounce of forgiveness had evaporated from the hearts of black people. That hatred for those who caused their suffering would be passed down through the generations. Instead, something profound took place. Millions of black people forgave.

As time passed the issue of equal rights digressed as other social issues like women's suffrage and labor laws for children grew more important. Because the movement of equal rights was so young it was easy for people to go back to their old ways of thinking when dark skin was synonymous to slavery. Consequently, equality for blacks remained out of reach.

As the world entered the 20th century, an explosion in European immigration took place in America. Assimilation for these immigrants was merely a matter of dropping a last name or dismissing a culture in order to meld into society. Unlike blacks who after centuries of laboring to help build the nation could not gain acceptance. Their skin color forever differentiated them. Interestingly enough most African Americans have no issue with their skin color. In fact, they continue to look for ways to embrace it. More relevant still, they have built a rich culture around their skin color, which resonates cross-culturally around the world. The ongoing struggle for African Americans is finding their identity within the confines of American society. As more information is learned about their rich heritage no doubt they will wear their skin color, even more so, like a badge of honor respective to all.

# THE AFTERWORD

We have peered into the mirror of our past less obscured to gain a better understanding about why we believe what we believe about race. Realizing also, how detrimental such constructs are to a society and the heavy price we all pay for our duplicity.

*The cost of slavery in America?*

Countless millions of lives were destroyed by the institution of slavery. Freedom for slaves had resulted in the Civil War whereby one-half million people died. Such an extreme loss of life however, was not sufficient enough to bring about equal rights under the law. Equality was impeded by superior and inferior ideals that were coming to fruition.

What then, would equality cost us?

As nations in the west expanded their reach into foreign lands, they carried with them notions of superior and inferior races, contaminating populations around the world. Again, what would be the cost of equality? In addition, what price would the world have to pay for the propagation of superior and inferior races? Let us move forward on our journey.

# Chapter VI

# Global Spread
of Race

# SCRAMBLE FOR AFRICA

A considerable number of events had taken place since West African trade caravans crossed the Sahara. England had risen to world power. The Trans-Atlantic Slave Trade had removed vast millions of people out of Africa. America was a fledgling nation and the Civil War had decided the fate of slavery. Another crucial change in the world was the creation of a racial paradigm based on skin color. By now, the West African empire was merely a blur from the past. Yet the abundance of wealth contained within its regions was of primary interest to leaders in Western Europe, even to the extent of the entire continent. To them, Africa was like a huge smorgasbord wide open for the taking. So began the scramble for Africa.

Many western economies had changed from agriculture to industry, which meant there was a constant need of raw materials for manufacturing. Western leaders also desired natural riches, especially gold; for they believed that the nation possessing the greatest amount, stood at the pinnacle of all nations of the world. Thus, the main objective for these leaders became "he who holds the gold holds the power." Their want to attain such wealth sparked unparalleled competition as they hurried to occupy Africa. At the time, no international authorities such as the League of Nations or United Nations existed and thus no one intervened, which left Africa up for grabs. Adding credence to their actions was the notion of superior and inferior races.

Now, the British had always relied upon foreign imports to supply materials for manufacturing, which placed them in a position of dependency upon other lands. What they wanted however was to be self-sufficient. To achieve this goal they needed to build a substantial reserve of raw materials. They also wanted to build up a national treasure in gold, diamonds, and other natural riches, all of which could be found in Africa. This placed the continent squarely within the crosshairs of the British Empire. Under the authority of a national policy which was "for reasons of commercial security," the British invaded Africa. Moving swiftly, they began to colonize regions known to be storehouses in gold, diamonds and other valuable resources. Yet, there were other options available to the British. Places lying dormant in which they could have occupied and utilized. Still they preferred Africa and other lands with a ready workforce.

Hardly was it the best time to re-invade Africa considering that the people were still reeling from the effects of having millions abstracted from the land because of slavery. Family members left behind called their loved ones "the disappeared". This extraordinary loss broke the spirit of the people. Even the land seemed to have lost its vitality. Now there was barely a pause between the end of slavery and this second invasion. This time the people remained in the land but under the brutal authority of the British Empire. Establishing laws that paralleled those practiced within the institution of slavery, the British denied Africans of their basic human rights and forced them into a perpetual state of poverty. They would not afford Africans a good education, adequate housing, or decent jobs. In fact, no development of an African society took place and the British thwarted their every effort to gain better treatment. Whatever good thing the British found, they set aside for themselves; and, as they stripped the land clean, they stored up huge stockpiles of raw materials in England.

# EMPIRE FOR EMPIRE SAKE

By the late 1800's western rivalries over Africa's riches had grown tense. To calm these rising disputes in 1884, leaders came together at the Conference of Berlin to decide how they would split up Africa; and, as a lioness divvies up prey to her cubs, Africa was sectioned off with the British receiving the lion's share. Yet after the Conference of Berlin some leaders were still unhappy and thus, Africa continued to be an issue. As western nations began to take control over Africa, great resistance came from the Ashante, Tsustu, Zulu and Mandinka warriors who in massive numbers withstood their invasion, at least for a while. But ten-foot spears and the most precise archery could not hold up against European firepower. Ethiopia would be the only African nation to withstand Italy's first attempt to invade. The British continued their domination over lands in India, China and Latin America. They added to the British Commonwealth, Newfoundland, Canada, Australia, New Zealand and South Africa. Their reach became so vast that the British could say, "The sun never sets on the British Empire." Moreover, wherever their feet treaded, they set down rules of superior and inferior humans.

After gutting Africa and other lands of vital resources, they had stockpiled enough raw materials so that they no longer relied upon foreign imports. Finally, their objective of becoming a self-sustaining empire was realized. After gaining control over much of the world's raw materials, they moved to monopolize world trade. They easily out manufactured all other competing nations to become the "marketplace of the world." The British routinely undersold their products to beat out competition from other nations and offered free trade agreements to nations with growing economies, which was something no other nation could afford to offer. British stronghold on international trade was so staggering that at one point they produced one-half of all the manufactured goods in the United States and other western lands. Still, the British Empire was not satisfied and continued to seize more lands around the world. A national policy that was initially for "reasons of commercial security" could now only be described as out-and-out greed. Their cupidity and over consumption caused them to put into place yet another national policy that read "Empire for empire's sake," giving them the authority to take whatever they desired.

It seemed that Darwin's foretelling of world dominance by the *superior race* was actually taking place.

All told, the number of colonies under British rule represented real estate in every hemisphere on earth and to keep the control over these lands they put forth a tremendous military force. In the interest of the British Empire, two hundred and fifty thousand soldiers were spread around the world.

While the Empire was preoccupied with colonization neighboring nation/states such as Germany began to build up a military force of their own. It was only less than a century earlier that Germany had consisted of merely a few loosely related states with no central government but by the beginning of the 20th Century, it was a rapidly growing nation. The German people were highly skilled at manufacturing so they quickly became competitive in global trade. The British, determined to hold on to their number one position, put into place more restrictive trade policies to hinder Germany and other industrialized nations from competing. Their actions were so extreme that the leaders of nations began to mount formal complaints against the British Empire. In Germany, leaders accused the British of undermining the world trade system and described them as, "A decadent empire holding in feeble hands, one quarter of the earth in fee."

# RUDIMENTS OF WAR

By the early 1900's, the British had amassed a net worth of eighty billion dollars, which by today's standards is equivalent to multiple trillions. What's more, the empire had grown to include twenty-five percent of the world's total population. Now the challenge was to maintain its position as "the workshop of the world." The United States and Germany however, were in hot pursuit. About a decade into their efforts the U.S. had reached number one in international trade and the Germans tied with the British for second place. These results only intensified the rivalry between the British and the Germans. In addition, there was concern among the nations that the British were stockpiling weapons and building up their military forces. Under pressure from these nations the British agreed to make concessions by easing their more restrictive trade policies and reducing weaponry production. Their actions had little effect on the Germans, who continued to build up their military strength and within four short years, Germany had doubled its army and naval forces. Friction between western nations continued to grow until tensions culminated into war, which spread to other parts of

Europe and then the world. So began World War I. Germany sided with nations that opposed the British and their allies. The war ended in defeat for the Germans who suffered the greatest number of casualties. To punish them for their role in the war, the British along with its allies, demanded that they pay reparations totaling in the billions of dollars. The amount was excessive. Too much for German people to re-pay but they had no other choice. With war debt hanging over them it seemed that the German economy would never recover. Unemployment soared. From town to town, breadlines stretched for miles because of food shortages and basic essentials like soap were scarce. The Germans desperately needed a strong leader to guide them and lift their economic burdens. That leader would be Hitler. He led the German people out of desperate times into a realm of success they had never known before. He was masterful at responding to their exigencies, as such, he quickly became the favorite among the people. Under his leadership, people had good paying factory jobs and the economy stabilized. Food lines disappeared and there was plenty of good soap and other goods. Yes, times were better for the German people so they willingly acceded to his leadership. Hitler relished in their trust for he was a cunning opportunist, presenting himself as the optimal defender of Germany and yet, few of them knew what he was truly planning. His deceit was so well hidden that most Germans went about their daily lives as unwitting participants in his sinister plan. Hitler's elaborate goal was to build a master race of German people, to shape Germany into a world power and ultimately build an empire for the "Third Reich." *Sound familiar?* It was as if Hitler were reading a *how to* manual for British imperialism. He probably would have never admitted it but many of his ideas mirrored those of the British Empire. He wanted what they had achieved while at the same time, despised the British, blaming them for Germany's problems. As the British had followed the footsteps of Rome, Hitler studied the path of the British Empire. He embraced the same race science, as had the Englishman Darwin, decades earlier. In his book, *Mein Kampf*, Hitler repeated some of Darwin's ideals. Rather than a *superior race* as Darwin assigned to the British, Hitler touted the Germans as a *master race*. Darwin however, stopped just shy of calling for the extinction of the *lower races*, leaving it up to evolution to do the job. Yet, Hitler was too impatient for evolution to kick in; and instead, he devised a plan to rid the world of the so-called inferior races within his own lifetime. In the hands of madness, the notion of superior and inferior races had reached the depths of evil.

Hitler applied the same psychological conditioning to the German people as had other western nations. He used the media, social organizations, educational system, as well as the church to disseminate a message of supremacy. As a result, he garnered an unwavering support from the German people. He created a xenophobic attitude that was unparalleled. It was marked by a droid-like appeal for Hitler and a deep-seated loathing for other people. The notion of superior and inferior humans had once again, worked. The mantra for Germany became *Ein Volk, ein Reich, ein, Fuhrer!* "One people, One empire, One leader!" Hitler was now poised to "Conquer for Germany the rank of world power." By the time the German people realized his ominous plans it was too late. The monster was unleashed. Hitler moved to cut off Germany from the rest of the world isolating the people from all outside contact. Then he began to reveal the wicked elements of his plan and suddenly Germany became a very dangerous place. The wonderful changes that had taken place were gone. *The good soap disappeared.* Anyone opposing his views ended up in concentration camps so they could *re-think* their position. Too often, they were killed in cold blood. Hitler applied the process of depuration to the weakest among his own people. By murdering them, he sought to cleanse his race of impurities. Hitler's pogroms were mostly directed toward the Jews as he systematically murdered at least six million people, almost wiping out the entire population; and his murdering spree continued with others who he deemed to be inferior. The world choked upon these horrors.

*"He who would live must fight. He who does not wish to fight in the world, where permanent struggle is the law of life has not the right to exist."* – Adolph Hitler, *Mein Kampf*

Hitler's attempt to build a master race and to conquer the world for German supremacy pushed the nations into a second world conflict. World War II would end in yet another defeat for Germany. Rather than face his perceived enemies Hitler chose the coward's way out, spending his last days hiding like a badger beneath the earth. But his attempt to force upon the world an ideal of superior and inferior races would demand requiting. World War II resulted in the death of **sixty million** people, not including the mass murdering of **millions** of innocent civilians.

# IN RETROSPECT

At least **sixty million** people dead. An unconscionable amount. To put into perspective, it would be like wiping out the entire Western Coast of America. This includes all the people living in California, Oregon and Washington as well as Arizona, Nevada and Utah. One can only wonder if after witnessing such a tremendous loss of life if there was enough contrition. Were lessons learned and passed along to future generations or will we find ourselves in the future, drinking from the same ole' watering trough.

At the end of World War II, the British Empire had earned a measure of culpability from which they could not escape. Early on, they had planted and nurtured ideals of superior and inferior races. They were the ones who developed a racial agenda. Now, after banking two world wars, much of the wealth was gone. The British Empire, strapped for cash, could no longer maintain its sizeable military presence in foreign lands. As their power and authority waned, India seized the opportunity to resist their occupation. India was followed by Egypt, which regained its independence first. Then India, through a non-violent movement led by Mohandas Gandhi, gained its independence. The countries of Ghana, Sierra Leone, Tanganyika, Uganda, Kenya, Zanzibar, Gambia, Botswana, Lesotho and Swaziland followed. Slowly, Africa was regaining its independence.

The lifeline of the ambitious British Empire, was short-lived, lasting less than a century. Known as Great Britain today, its wealth has declined to such a degree that it is no longer the preeminent world power as it was before. Yet the implication of race, which the British helped to spread around the world, still influences us today.

# FINAL WORDS

So have we made strides in the area of race? Well, yes we have. Decades after World War II, federal laws superseded local Black Codes and Jim Crow laws that deprived people of fair treatment. These new laws were made to govern every American. Without exception, laws are only as good as the people who make them but when laws are justly applied, everyone wins. Still, no law is greater than the choices we make - a fact made evident throughout our journey. For slavery as well as the notion of superior and inferior races were matters of choice. We must take ownership of that truth.

Besides changes in our laws, great strides in science have also taken place. Remarkably, since the days of Darwin, advanced science disproves the racial science that prevailed throughout much of the last century. Today the consensus among anthropologist coincides with what people living outside of our racial constructs have always known. We are more alike than we are different.

*"In the United States both scholars and the general public*

*have been conditioned to viewing human races as natural and separate divisions within the human species based on visible physical differences. With the vast expansion of scientific knowledge in this century, however, it has become clear that human populations are not unambiguous, clearly demarcated, biologically distinct groups. "-* American Anthropological Association Statement on "Race" May 17, 1998

The science of DNA gives us additional proof that humans share most of the same traits. Using DNA science, the Human Genome Project, a thirteen-year international research program, discovered that 99.9% of all the genetic material that makes us human is **identical**. This means that less than one percent of our makeup is different. And within this sliver of a percentage resides skin color. It is truly astounding how much hate we have managed to pack into such a small measure and how detrimental this choice has been to humanity. In addition, there is the propensity for an oppressed group after gaining strength to become the *oppressor*. Clearly, these matters reveal to us that as humans, we continue to struggle in areas of compassion and tolerance. This tells us that the evolution that needs to take place is not in our physical bodies but rather, it is the evolution of the heart, grounded in love. As simplistic as this may sound, pure love is the most powerful tool in the universe for love is not weak and it does not oppress. Love is intolerant of evil and it seeks justice for all. It has no preference to skin color. Love is undeniably, a state of evolution that people in the world have yet to attain.

In spite of our past, the freedoms that we embrace as Americans have allowed us, through trial and error, to become better. We are the only nation in the world that beckons other lands to "Give me your tired, your poor, your muddled masses yearning to breathe free." It is an invitation to every creed, skin color, religion and national origin to come to our beautiful shores—the very thing that makes us strong for we are a glorious tapestry of creativity and ingenuity. May the hearts of all Americans continue to *evolve*. We shall do well toward that end and anything less we must make obsolete.

SKIN- 185 -

# BIBLIOGRAPHY

## Chapter I / The Makings of an Ideal

Santayana, George. *Reason in Common Sense.* (Dover
   Publishing 1980)

## Chapter II / Lost Ages of Africa

Africanus, Leo and Dr. K. Molefi. *Classical Africa*
   (Peoples Publication Group, 1994)

Akkadian Semitic Languages. (2007) Retrieved from
   http://phoenicia.org/alphabet.html

Austen, Ralph A. *Trans-Saharan Africa in World History*
   (USA: Oxford University Press, 2010). Ch. II 36, 43
   and Ch. III 53,54

Barth, Heinrich and Locke Ward. *Travels and discoveries in
   North and Central Africa: including accounts of Tripoli,
   the Sahara, the remarkable kingdom of Bornu, and the
   countries around Lake Chad* (1890)

Bender, Lionel M. et al. *Language in Ethiopia* (UK: Oxford
   Univ. Press, 1976)

Burton, Richard F. *First Footsteps in East Africa: Or an Exploration of Harari* (Longman, Brown, Gree & Longmans, 1856)

"Petrie Museum Traveling Exhibit of Egypt." Carlos C. Michaels Museum. Emory University, Atlanta, GA. 2010

Cavalli-Sforza, Luigi L., Paolo Menozzi, and Alberto Piazza. *The History & Geography of Human Genes* (NJ: Princeton University Press, 1994) 163

CIA FACTBOOK. Retrieved from https://www.cia.gov/library/publications/the-world-factbook/

Conrad, David C. *Empires of Medieval West Africa - Great Empires of the Past* (Facts on File, 2005)

De Lafayette, Maximillien *Akkadian-English Dictionary Comparative Lexicon of Akkadian, Sumerian, Assyrian, Babylonian, Chaldean, Phoenician, Ugaritic, Hittite, Aramaic and Syriac.* (NY: Times Square Press, 2011)

Diakonoff, Igor M. *Historical Comparative Vocabulary of Afrasian* (Undena Publishing, 1993-1997) 2-6

Ehrel, Christopher. *Reconstructing Proto-Afroasiatic (Pro-Afrasian): Vowels, Tone Consonants & Vocabulary – Voices from Asia* (CA: University of California Press, 1995) 72

GA Public Broadcasting, Nova. "Ancient Egyptian
    Pyramid." Retrieved from
    http://www.pbs.org/wgbh/nova/pyramid/explore/age.ht
    ml

Greenberg, Joseph H. *Studies in African Linguistic
    Classification: IV, Hamito-Semitic*, Southwestern
    Journal of Anthropology 6 (Smithsonian Institute,
    1950)

General Editor - Gowing, Lawrence *A History of Art* (Barnes
    & Noble Books, 1995) 19, 25, 28

Hayward, Richard J.; Edited by Heini Bernd and Nurse,
    Derek *An introduction in Afroasiatic: African
    Languages* (Cambridge Univ. Press, 2000), 74-98

Hetzron, Robert, ed. *The Semitic Languages,
    Routledge Language Family Series* (NY: Routledge
    Taylor & Frances Group, 1997), 3-15

Jeffrey, S.B., ed. *A Guide to Ancient Egyptian History*
    (Webster's Digital Services, 2011) 15

McNaughton, Parick R. *The Mande Blacksmiths: Knowledge,
    Power, & Art in West Africa* (First Midland Book
    Edition, 1993), 38

Moore, Francis; Stibbs, Bartholomew and Africanus, Leo
    *Travels into the inland parts of Africa: Containing a
    description of the several nations for the space of six*

*hundred miles up the River Gambia* (Nabu Press, 2nd ed., 2010) 66 -68

National Geographic News. " Timbuktu." Retrieved from http://news.nationalgeographic.com/news/2003/05/photogalleries/timb

Owens, Jonathan. *A Linguistic History of Arabic* (USA: Oxford University Press, 2009) 72

Reiner, Erica *A Linguistic Analysis of Akkadian* (Mouton & Company, 1966)

Robinson, Andrew. *The Story of Writing: Alphabets, Hieroglyphs, & Pictograms* (Thames & Hudson 2nd edition, 2007) 13

Ruhlens, Merrit. *On the Origin of Language: Tracing the Evolution of the Mother Tongue* (John Wiley & Sons, Inc., 1994), 24-25 and 42

**Chapter III / Early English Times**

Black Death. Retrieved from http://www.jewishhistory.org/the-black-death/

Boccaccio, Giovanni. *The Decameron* (Library of Princeton University) 12

Daichman, Graciela S. *Wayward Nuns in Medieval Literature* (NY: Syracuse Univ. Press, 1986) 2-3, 54, 56 and 622

Durant, Will. *The Reformation – The Story of Civilization VI* (NY: Simon & Schuster, 1957) 17

Howarth, David. 1066: *Year of Conquest* (USA: Vikings Penguin, 1977) 14

Jacobsthal, Paul. *Early Celtic Art* (UK: Mandrake Press)

Jimenez, Ramon. *Caesar Against the Celts* (DA Capo Press, 1996) 36

Johnson, Cuthbert W. *The Farmer's Encyclopedia and Dictionary of Rural Affairs* (Longman, Brown, Green & Longmans, 1842) 439

Malaterra, Geoffrey and Wolf, Baxter K. *The Deeds of Count Roger of Calabria Sicily and His Brother Duke Robert Guisc* (MI: University of Michigan Press, 2005) 52

Tacitus, Cornelius and Anthony A. Barrett. Translated by Yardley, J.C. *The Annals: the Reigns of Tiberius, Claudius and Nero* (USA: Oxford Univ. Press, 2008) 250, 319.

UK History Learning. (2004). Retrieved from http://www.historylearningsite.co.uk

## Chapter V / The Pupil

Aptheker, Herbert. *American Negro Slave Revolts* (Int. Publications, 5th ed., 1983) 21

Byrd, William. "The Secret Diaries of William Byrd of Westover 1709-1712." (2007). Retrieved from http://www.pbs.org/wgbh/aia/part1/1h283t.html

A Chronology of Antislavery: 18th Century. Retrieved from www.digitalhistory.uh.edu/historyonline/antis/chron

Carretta, Vincent. *Phyllis Wheatley: Biography of a Genius in Bondage* (GA: Sahara Mills Hodge Fund Publication, Univ. of GA Press, 2011)160

Cole, Thomas. "Sketches of the Santee River." *American Monthly Magazine,* (1836)

Conrad, Earl. *Harriet Tubman: Negro Soldier and Abolitionist* (N.Y.: Int. Publishers, 1942) 40

Darwin, Charles and General Editor - Quammen, David *On The Origin of Species by Means of Natural Selection* (USA, London: Sterling Publishing, 2008) Ch. IV - 128; Ch. V - 130, 138-139, 146-147; Ch. VI - 163; Ch. VII – 189

Darwin, Charles. *The Descent of Man* (NY: Prometheus Books, 1998) Ch III - 96, 97

DeBois, Filix. *Timbuctoo the Mysterious* (Nabu Press, 2010) 285

Douglass, Frederick. *Narrative of the Life of Frederick Douglass* (USA: Simon & Brown, 2012) 13,14,27,83

Douglass, Frederick and Harriet Jacobs. *Narrative of the Life of Frederick Douglass, an American Slave & Incidents in the Life of a Slave Girl* (Modern Library, 2004) 132, 271

Douglass Frederick. *Selected Addresses of Frederick Douglass – An African American Heritage Book.* (Wilder Publications, 2008) 30

Drafted Men Recruits and Substitutes 1864-1865. RG 110 Provost Marshal General Bureau (Civil War) KY

Edited by Chapman, Abraham *Black Voices an Anthology of African American Literature* (NY: New American Library, Penguin Putnam, Inc., 1968)

Edited by Hall, G. Stanley and George H. Blakeslee. *The Journal of the Race Development,* (MA: Clark University, Vol. I, 1910-1911) 489

Equiano, Olaudah and Vincent Carretta. *The Interesting Narrative and Other Writings* (Penguin Classics, Rev. ed. 2003) 60, 111

Frances, Anika. "The Economics of the African Slave

Trade." Retrieved from  http://ebookbrowse.com/
anika-francis- the-economics-of-the-african-slave-
trade-pdf-d264735409

GA Public Television. "Africans in America." Retrieved
from  http://www.pbs.org/wgbh/aia/part2/index.html

Glen, James and, Elizabeth A. Donnan. *Description of South
Carolina* (USA: Octagon Books, 1965)

Gibbons, William Jr. Papers: *"Bill of Sale for Nan"* (NC: GA
Special Collections, Duke University Library)

Governor Glen & Dr. Milligen, George *South Carolina: Two
Contemporary Descriptions* (USA: Johnston, 1951)

Harris, Robert L, et al. *African American
History in The Press.* (1851-1899). (NY: Gale
Publishing, 1996) 28,312

Jefferson, Thomas *Letter to Roger C. Weightman, Mayor of
Washington D.C., Repository* (Washington D.C.:
Library of Congress Rare Book and Special Collections
Division, Broadside Collection) Portfolio 186, no. 2 c-
Rare Book

Le Jau, Frances. *St. James's Parish, Goose Creek, Letter to
Society* (Library of Congress Transcript, Series, 390-
395; as printed in Klingberg's Le Jau [1956], 53-56.
SPG series A, volume IV, 478-481)

Lincoln, Abraham. *Collected Works of Abraham Lincoln 1858* (Wildside Press, 2008)

Lincoln, Abraham. *Letter to Albert Hodges – 1864* (U.S. Library of Congress, American Treasures)

Lincoln, Abraham *Letter to Honorable Horace Greeley – 1862* (U.S. Library of Congress)

Lincoln, Abraham Lincoln: Speeches & Writings: 1859-1865 (Library of America, 1989) 628

Manigault, Louis *Names of New Hands at Gowrie & East Hermitage – 1860* (NC: Duke University Library)

Marshall, Peter and Manuel, David *Sounding Forth the Trumpet: 1837-1860* (Revell, 1999) 358

Miles, Johnnie H., et al. *Afro-American Almanac – African American History Res. 1865* (USA: Jossey-Bass, 2000) 35

Minneapolis Federal Reserve Bank. "Inflation Calculator." Retrieved from www.dot.minneapolisfed.org

National Archives Southeastern Region, U. S. Union Army Descriptive Book of Colored Drafted Men, Recruits, and Substitutes, RG 110 Provost Marshal General Bureau, Civil War Kentucky, 1864-1865.

National Archives Southeastern Region, GA: 1800's Map of

GA Census, 2010 Exhibit.

Ohio Historical Society. (2005). Retrieved from
http://www.ohiohistorycnetral.org

Pre-civil War Free States vs. Slave States. (2010). Retrieved
from http://sensoryoverload.typepad.com

Shaw, Flora. *A Tropical Dependency, An Outline of the
Ancient History of the Western Soudan with an Account
of Modern Settlement of Northern Nigeria* (NY:
Cambridge University Press, 1905) 283.

Smith, Sir Thomas."DeRepublica Anglorum." Retrieved
from   http://www.tanos.org.uk/quotations

Smithsonian Institute. "Human Origins Program." Retrieved
from http://humanorigins.si.edu/

Smithsonian Institute American History Documents Gallery.
"Lincoln, Abraham." (2004). Retrieved from
http://americanhistory.si.edu/documentsgallery/exhibitions/Americas
new_birth_of_freedom_3.html

Strickland, Matthew. *War and Chivalry: The conduct and
Perception of War in England* 1066-1217 (UK:
Cambridge University Press, 1996) 307.

Ta'Rikh, Al-Sa'Di. Edited by John O. Hunwick, *Timbuktu
and the Songhay Empire: Al-Sa'Di's Ta'Rikh Al-Sudan
Down to 1613 and Other Contemporary Documents*

(Brill Academic Publications, 2003).

Thompson, Elizabeth L. *The Reconstruction of Southern Debt: Bankruptcy After the Civil War* (GA: University of Georgia Press, 2004) Chapter I – 14

Walvin, James. *Slavery & the Slave Trade – A Short Illustrated History* (MS: Univ. Press, 1983).

Wilson, B. *The Black Codes of the South* (AL: University of Alabama Press, 1965.

Wilson, Marcius. *American History--Comprising historical sketches of the Indian tribes: A Description of American Antiquities* (MI: University of Michigan Libraries, Mark H. Newman & Co. New York, 1847) Book II - 140, appendices to the period.

U.S. Library of Congress. "Voices of Slaves."(2004). Retrieved from http://memory.loc.gov/ammem /snhtml/snintro02.htm

## Chapter VI / Global Spread of Race

American Anthropological Association (2200 Wilson Blvd, Suite 600, Arlington, VA 22201) http://www.aaanet.org

Marshall, Logan *A History of The Nations And Empires Involved And A Study of The Events Culminating In The*

*Great Conflict* (Kessinger Publishing, LLC, 2010) 22, 44, 45, 47, 51.

Office of Biological Environmental Research, U.S. Dept. of Energy Office of Science. "Human Genome Project." (2007) Retrieved from http://genomics.energy.gov/

U.S. Census Bureau. "Resident Population; State Statistics." (2010). Retrieved from http://www.census.gov/

**Resources:**

1. Clayton County Library Galileo (Jonesboro, GA)
2. Columbia Encyclopedia, Columbia University Press, 6th. Edition, 2003
3. Edward W. Goodrick and John R Kohlenberger, NIV Exhaustive Concordance Holy Bible, King James
4. Encyclopedia Britannica (2003)
5. Fulton County Library Resource Center (Atlanta, GA)
6. Funk & Wagnalls New Encyclopedia
7. MSN Encarta
8. New Georgia Encyclopedia, University of GA Press
9. Torah (The Jewish Publication Society)

## ABOUT THE AUTHOR

A. P. Brooks was born in Atlanta, Georgia and grew up during the 60's and 70's. At a very young age, her mother introduced books into the home. Not just ordinary books for children but books that exposed her to different cultures and people, allowing her to explore the world without leaving the bedroom. She was perfectly satisfied occupying a space surrounded by reading materials from Archie comics to the history of Beethoven. This love of books sparked an interest in writing and her unique style revealed a talent for extracting emotion from words. Recognizing this talent, her elementary school teacher submitted one of her poems to a national magazine for children. In college, she continued her life course in writing by studying journalism. Most of her adult career has been in marketing and sales; most notably, she completed a special project on behalf of the U.S. First Lady, Laura Bush, in April 2008. The book *SKIN* is a culmination of years of research and writing that has taken Mrs. Brooks on her own personal journey of healing and discovery. Her Christian faith, wonderful husband, two children, and two grandchildren are the center of her life.

DISCARD

17435411R00124

Made in the USA
Charleston, SC
11 February 2013